THE MAYOS
Pioneers in Medicine

The story of the Mayos—Dr. William, the father, and his sons, Dr. Will and Dr. Charlie—spans a century of medical progress from the frontier days of Minnesota where a sick cow was Dr. William's first patient to the solemnity of the operating room in their own clinic; from the excitement of tornadoes and racing special trains to the humanitarian deeds of two great surgeons who loved their fellow men, and to the story of the world-famous Mayo Clinic at Rochester, Minnesota.

THE MAYOS

Pioneers in Medicine

By ADOLPH REGLI

ILLUSTRATED BY RAFAELLO BUSONI

Julian Messner, Inc.

NEW YORK

PUBLISHED BY JULIAN MESSNER, INC.
8 WEST 40TH STREET, NEW YORK

PRINTED IN THE UNITED STATES OF AMERICA
BY MONTAUK BOOK MANUFACTURING CO., INC.

Contents

I.	A COW FOR A PATIENT	3
II.	AN INDIAN WAR BREWS	15
III.	DR. MAYO CALLED TO WAR	25
IV.	DOCTOR TURNS INDIAN FIGHTER	32
V.	THE MAYO SKELETON	43
VI.	THOSE MAYO BOYS	52
VII.	AN ANESTHETIST AT TWELVE	65
VIII.	MERCY RIDES A TORNADO	75
IX.	HOSPITAL RUN ON UNIQUE POLICY	87
X.	TOO MUCH MONEY FOR TWO	95
XI.	THE MAYO REPUTATION EXPANDS	105
XII.	SURGICAL TWINS ALMOST PARTED	118
XIII.	THEY PICKED THE RIGHT PARENTS	126
XIV.	THEY GIVE AWAY A FORTUNE	136
XV.	MAYOS SERVE THEIR COUNTRY IN WAR	144
XVI.	A TWENTY-TWO-STORY DOCTORS' OFFICE	153
XVII.	WHAT THE MAYO BROTHERS WERE LIKE	164
XVIII.	THE DOCTORS SPEAK	178
XIX.	SONS HONOR FATHER AND MOTHER	194

Contents

XX.   BROTHERS HONORED BY NATION   200

XXI.   TRAGEDY AND DEATH   207

XXII.   THEY BUILT A CITY   215

XXIII.   HONORS FOR THE HONORABLE   221

BIBLIOGRAPHY   233

INDEX   241

THE MAYOS

Pioneers in Medicine

CHAPTER ONE

A Cow for a Patient

SQUAT, RUGGED MAN, HIS round face glistening with perspiration, hammered energetically on a row of cedar shingles spread across the roof of his new house. With movements deft and sure, he tacked the thin boards to the rough pine planks, pausing occasionally to dry his brow with a red handkerchief.

A gray haze in the west, rising to meet the gathering thunderheads, bore a prophecy of cooling rain. But for another hour the torturing summer sun would blister the gables of the small, two-story cottage that had taken its place on the edge of the pioneer village of Le Sueur, Minnesota.

From his perch atop the west gable that would protect his and Louise's bedroom, the man could see the uncoiling

Minnesota River, flat and silvery between the rolling prairies heavy with wheat.

The man on the roof stopped to appraise the green countryside, just emerging from its virgin state. There, almost opposite the village, was the Drake place. Farther downstream was the Lattimore farm and just in sight to the west was the Tousley farmstead.

On those very meadows beyond the river the Le Sueur house builder had tried his hand at farming, and had admitted defeat. To himself he quickly acknowledged this verdant land was not at fault. It was in the heart of a fine region, a great region. Of that he was sure. Otherwise, why had he decided to make it his home?

The memory of his first three years in this raw Northwest—three severe, sometimes desperate years—could not be erased overnight, however. He had come unprepared for the uncertainties of this woods-and-prairie outpost. He was a professional man, and the adjustment to the brutal life of a wilderness was not easy for him.

He had tried first to earn a living at St. Paul, next on the Lake Superior iron and copper range, then on a homestead near St. Peter. It was a vain effort. And so he decided finally to build a house and make his home at Le Sueur. He would practice his profession and give the community what he could of his knowledge and skill.

As he gazed over the trees that crowded the easy slope cradling the river, he saw a man in a skiff put out from the opposite shore. He pulled across the stream with flowing, powerful strokes until lost from sight in the rich foliage that concealed the village landing.

The builder returned to his task of placing shingles over knotholes and uneven cracks. He must hurry to complete the job before the rain came. So intent was he upon his job that he failed to observe the boatman walking up the path from the river.

The tall, weather-reddened stranger stood in the litter of boards, lathes, and plaster that cluttered the cottage yard. He watched the swinging arm and listened to the chattering hammer for a minute. When it appeared that the shingler was going on indefinitely, he announced himself.

"Hello, up there! Are you going to finish the whole house before you take a breath?"

The man on the roof looked down, hammer poised. "How do you do, sir."

"I hope you'll excuse me for interrupting such a busy person, but I'd like to talk to you a minute. You're the new doctor, the Englishman, aren't you? Dr. Mayo?"

"That's correct. William Worrall Mayo, if you want the whole business. And you, sir, are . . . ?"

"Drake. Colonel J. L. Drake. I'm from just across the river. You can see my farm over the trees."

"I'm happy to know you, Colonel. Is there anything I can do for you?"

"Well, I reckon maybe there is. Let's see now. You're supposed to treat and cure humans, aren't you?"

"That's my profession, sir."

"Well then, if you can doctor human beings, you ought to be able to help a cow, a sick one."

Dr. Mayo laughed heartily despite the seriousness of his questioner. He finally said, "Well, Colonel, I've never had an opportunity to treat a cow, but if you're willing to take a chance on me, the cow ought to. I'll certainly do the best I can. It will be an interesting experiment."

"I don't want any experimenting, Doctor. She's a valuable animal and I can't afford to lose her. But she's mighty sick and I've got to have someone look at her."

"All right, sir. We'd better attend to her at once. I have no skiff, so I'll have to ride over with you. Just a minute, I'll be with you."

Slipping down the ladder nimbly, Dr. Mayo joined the colonel. He was a full head shorter than the worried farmer and his thinning brown hair, already receding from his high forehead, made him appear older than his thirty-nine years.

Without stopping to discard his worn overalls and blue shirt that bore damp marks under the suspenders, Dr. Mayo walked with Colonel Drake to a neighbor's home to obtain his medicine kit and then set out for the village square.

"We'd better get a quart of castor oil, Colonel," Dr. Mayo suggested. "Castor oil has straightened out more ailments, human and animal, than pink pills."

Their purchase made at the village pharmacy, the two walked to the river and boarded the colonel's skiff.

"You're new in these parts, Dr. Mayo," Drake said when their conversation lagged. "Do you expect to make a go of it here—practicing medicine, I mean?"

"Well, the field is wide open. You pioneers think you're a tough lot and can get along without much medicine. But there's a good deal of suffering that is unnecessary and it's the physician's job to relieve it."

"Ah, but this is a healthy country. You won't find much sickness in Minnesota. It's good for consumption."

"That's what your land promoters and big speculators are publicizing back East. There's a lot of truth in it, but doctors are necessary out here, nevertheless."

"Maybe. But I'm afraid you'll find out it's too healthy to keep many of you fellows in bread and butter."

"You certainly aren't pampering us, I can tell you. When I came to St. Paul from Indiana in Fifty-five, I found there wasn't much of a welcome for my profession. I had to go copper prospecting at first. Then I took up surveying and finally turned to farming. Tried it at St. Peter in Fifty-six, but picked the wrong homestead. The next year I moved up here and took a claim on your side of the river, but it didn't go any better."

"You've got to know how to farm the prairie."

"I've found out I'm no farmer. Last winter I ran out of feed for my eight head of oxen and I had to ask G. M. Tousley, my nearest neighbor, to help me out. He took them off my hands and saved them."

Dr. Mayo stopped talking and Colonel Drake rowed on without commenting. The doctor sat silent, thinking of the risks he had faced since leaving England to make his way in this untamed Northwest.

After bringing his wife and two small daughters from La Porte, Indiana, he had tried for three years to establish a home with some promise of security. In the wild river town of St. Paul, in the rugged Lake Superior ranges, on the broad plains of the Minnesota River valley the story had been the same. Failure. He had barely escaped with his life from the north woods. He had earned the scantiest of livings in a country that had promised happiness and plenty, come one, come all.

His chin hardened and the mellow lines of his ruddy face stiffened in determination. Dr. William Worrall Mayo, descendant of a family of physicians and surgeons who had made medical history in England, was not submitting to the trials of a new country. He was a fighter, beaten and battered, but not licked. And he was just beginning to fight.

He looked back at the village of Le Sueur, snuggling on the riverbank. It had been named after the seventeenth-century Frenchman, Pierre Charles Le Sueur, who had discovered the Minnesota River. Le Sueur was to be his home. In this year of our Lord 1858, he was building his own house. There he would soon move his family—his wife Louise and two daughters. There he would earn a livelihood. He would do it as a physician, to human beings or to animals, if need be. But as a physician he was determined to survive.

The skiff nosed gently against the sandy riverbank and Colonel Drake stepped ashore. "Well, Doctor, here we are. We'll find that sick critter in the shed at the right."

Dr. Mayo, carrying a quart of castor oil under his arm, started up the hill to attend his first patient as the doctor of Le Sueur. He cured Colonel Drake's ailing bovine and started on the road to professional success that was to lead directly to medicine's miracle: "The Clinic in the Cornfields," "The Medical Lodestone," "The Supreme Court of Condemned Patients."

Dr. Mayo's two sons, whose genius was to fashion an institution destined to become world-renowned as the Mayo Clinic of Rochester, Minnesota, were not yet born. But the background for their spectacular medical achievements was even then being laid by the little country doctor amid the unscarred woods and prairies of southern Minnesota.

The metal for their future humanitarian work was being tempered and drawn in the horrors of Indian massacres, in the very struggle for existence in a hostile, sometimes cruel, frontier region.

Only the strong and the able survived the rigors of such an era. Proof that William Worrall Mayo was one of the select is found in his realization of a vision that a monument to the medical profession should arise out of the skill and knowledge he could instill in his sons, William James and Charles Horace.

Long before he died at the age of ninety-two, Dr. Mayo helped to create the clinic that in its present operation advises and treats approximately one hundred thousand patients annually. He lived to see the ailing, the halt, and the suffering come from every nation to receive the healing touch of the "Mayo Boys." A richer reward for early struggles a father never received from faithful sons.

When Dr. Mayo cured Colonel Drake's cow, he did more than save a valued animal for a pioneer farmer. He won a grateful friend who spread the word of the little doctor's skill.

Soon many of the sick and injured of the countryside called at the small white cottage in Le Sueur or summoned the doctor to their sod huts, miles from the river and far off the dusty trails that served as roads in the Minnesota River valley. Usually by horseback, but often afoot, he made his calls. By day or night, in storm and sunshine, he answered every appeal. When friends and neighbors spoke of "The Doctor," there was no need for more identification. Dr. Mayo was "The Doctor" of the valley. For forty years he served as a country doctor and as such he remained to the last.

Too poor to set up an office in the village, Dr. Mayo crowded his desk, his medical books and scant scientific equipment into a tiny gabled room on the second floor of his home. Two large windows provided light for the physician's combination office and laboratory. The ceiling was so low a tall man could not stand erect in the room, yet it suited the short doctor perfectly. He had fashioned it for his own convenience. If it were too low for a visitor, let the visitor stoop.

Despite the impetus given his practice by the kind words of Colonel Drake, Dr. Mayo soon realized he could not rely solely on his profession to make a living. There was plenty of time for other pursuits in those first years at Le Sueur. Reverses came to him, just as they did to most of his neighbors. And like many of them, he turned to the river and its growing traffic to earn extra money.

Thus in his second year at Le Sueur, Dr. Mayo became "Captain" Mayo. With a small but sturdy riverboat, he moved supplies to settlers farther upstream and carried downriver to St. Paul their crops and timber. Competition was keen, however, and after a hard year of steamboating, Dr. Mayo gave it up and concentrated on his medicine.

He made one important contact as river captain, nevertheless. One client was a Jim Hill, a vigorous, farsighted promoter who later became famous in Northwest railroad history as James J. Hill, Empire Builder.

Dr. Mayo's friendship with the railroader was to cause, many years later, Dr. William James Mayo to break an ironclad rule never to operate outside of St. Mary's Hospital in Rochester. He hurried to St. Paul in 1916 to perform an emergency operation on the aging James Hill, but the Empire Builder was beyond medical aid.

The year 1861 was marked by two events that became major influences in the life of the little doctor. The first was the outbreak of the Civil War. Even in the remote frontier of Minnesota it had its devastating effects.

It brought, happily, some security to the Mayo household after the doctor was appointed examining surgeon for the provost marshal in charge of Army recruiting. Here was a little income, at least, that would provide food for the family. This, together with occasional fees collected for medical service to scattered patients, gave promise that Dr. Mayo could thereafter apply his uninterrupted time to the profession he loved and cherished.

The second milestone of that year of even greater moment than the Civil War to Dr. Mayo was the birth of his first son, William James, on June 29, 1861. He already was the father of three daughters, Gertrude Emily, Phoebe, and Sarah. Sarah died early in childhood, but Gertrude and Phoebe were vigorous and hardy youngsters when William's arrival enlarged the Mayo household.

Dr. Mayo was forty-two and his wife, Louise Abigail, thirty-six at the time of their son's birth. Their happiness was unbounded as they fondled their boy.

"He's a wonderful child, Louise dear," the doctor said as he sat at his wife's bedside holding her hand. "He'll be a credit to the Mayo name."

"I'm sure he will. Our prayers have been answered, William. He'll be as good a doctor as his father is."

"As good! He'll be far better, you'll see. He won't have the struggles we've gone through. This will be a great and settled country when he starts to practice and he'll have the advantages of the coming advances in medicine. He's going to be a great doctor, Louise."

Dr. Mayo strutted about Le Sueur a proud and happy man.

With the Mayo fortunes apparently brightening, an ominous shadow crept across the Minnesota River valley. Mutterings of discontent among the Sioux Indians, who far outnumbered the white settlers, started an undercurrent of uneasiness in the villages along the river.

Three years before, the Sioux had signed over to the Federal government millions of acres of rich prairie lands.

Only a part of the sums promised had been paid to them, they charged. To bring the difficulty to a crisis, they were growing hungry and desperate. The corn crop of 1861 failed and the Indians demanded that the traders extend to them credit for food. This they were refused.

Dr. Mayo came home from the village one summer evening with reports of the Sioux's restlessness. Making certain the children would not overhear, he talked quietly with Louise.

"The situation apparently is becoming alarming, my dear. The men in the village are talking of a possible outbreak and steps to meet it."

"Oh, William, is it as serious as that?"

"I'm afraid so. Before we came out here, some five years ago, the Sioux attacked Heron Lake, Minnesota, and several communities in Dickinson County, Iowa. They massacred quite a few persons, but the Army never was able to capture the offenders and punish them. The men are saying we may have another fight on our hands because those murderers weren't caught and brought to justice. The Indians think the whites are weak and afraid to retaliate."

Louise was silent for a moment. She looked into her husband's face with fear deep in her eyes. "Do you think it safe for you to ride on your trips so far from the settlement, William?"

"Oh, I don't think it's that dangerous. We'll be warned in time if the Indians go on the warpath. Army scouts will know about that. I've seen many Sioux lately, and while they're far from friendly, they're not openly hostile."

"William, you must be careful. Don't you think you'd better postpone your call to the Alberton home tomorrow? Mrs. Alberton isn't in serious condition, is she?"

"I really can't say yet. But I must call. I told them I would be back Friday and a doctor can't let a few bellyaching Indians stand in his way. Should Mrs. Alberton become worse, I would be at fault."

"Yes, I suppose you are right, dear. But you must return before dark."

Next day Dr. Mayo saddled his little brown mare and set out for the Alberton home nearly fifteen miles south of the river. He found the settler's wife almost well. He accepted the Albertons' invitation to lunch, rested a short time to chat with the family, and then started for Le Sueur.

Dr. Mayo was almost dozing in his saddle when he reached a small stream two miles from the village. His mount picked her way to a shallow ford and started to cross.

A wild, piercing yell from a clump of bushes at his left so startled the little doctor that he almost fell from his horse.

Whooping lustily, three half-clad Sioux Indians sprang from their hiding place on the riverbank. They charged upon the horseman. The mare reared in fright.

Clinging tightly to the reins, Dr. Mayo swung the animal broadside to the attacking redskins. "Get away, you drunken fools," he shouted. "What do you mean by frightening my horse?"

"Give us pony!" one Indian demanded. "We want pony." He grasped the bridle and started to pull the mare toward the bank.

Dr. Mayo kicked out viciously. He struck the Indian on the forearm, breaking his hold on the rein. He lashed back at another with his riding whip. It fell across a bare shoulder with a crack.

"Take that, Cut Nose, you scoundrel!" Dr. Mayo cried

at the only one of the trio he recognized. "I'll teach you to leave my horse alone, you thieving rascal."

Battling like a demon, he kicked and whipped his way free of the Sioux. His horse plunged through the water, up the opposite bank. Dr. Mayo escaped without losing a bottle from his medicine kit, clutched in his shaking hand. He galloped home, certain now that trouble was in store for the white settlers of the Minnesota River valley.

That trouble was not far distant. It was to be accompanied by such ferocity and violence that it would carve a black page in the history of the Minnesota frontier.

Burned farms, defenseless settlers massacred—hundreds of them; pitched battles and savage treachery, flaming fields, heroism and hangings: these were to be the tragic episodes of the day.

Dr. Mayo was to share prominently in this outbreak of savage tempers against the westward march of the whites. He, and later his sons, William and Charles, were to have a great deal more to do with the ruthless Cut Nose he had just beaten off at the river ford.

CHAPTER TWO

An Indian War Brews

SOME MONTHS AFTER HIS brush with the three drunken Sioux at the ford, Dr. Mayo was riding his pony along the river road that skirted the village of Le Sueur. As he neared the landing, he observed Colonel Drake, the farmer whose cow he had saved, helping his wife and three children ashore from their skiff.

When still some distance away, he noted the grave demeanor of the parents and the half-frightened air about the children. It puzzled the doctor.

"Good afternoon, Colonel . . . Mrs. Drake. No more sick animals need attention today, I trust," he said jokingly.

"Hello, Doctor." Colonel Drake spoke almost without looking up. The curt greeting surprised Dr. Mayo. He watched the worried farmer a moment.

"Just a minute, Colonel," he said with some concern. "What's wrong? Is there trouble afoot?"

"Plenty. You've heard the Sioux have demanded a council at Fort Ridgely, haven't you?"

"Yes, of course. But the agents and traders will straighten things out, don't you think?"

"They could, and they may, but I have my fears. In fact, I believe the tribe is out of hand and there is going to be serious trouble hereabouts. I'm so concerned about it that I'm taking no chances. I'm moving my family into the village for safety."

"Really, Colonel! You're setting a bad example for the neighboring farmers. You may create a state of panic among them."

"I've seen redmen on the warpath and I can tell you, Doctor, I won't expose my family to their wrath. We can't afford to grow careless. The Indians are hungry, and a hungry Indian is a dangerous Indian. The traders aren't likely to give them either charity or credit. It's bad medicine."

Dr. Mayo rode home thoughtfully. He was well aware of the Sioux's grievances. They had signed a treaty on July 17, 1858, whereby the United States Senate had agreed to purchase from them vast tracts of land in Minnesota. The land, well worth five dollars an acre, was to be paid for at the rate of thirty cents an acre.

The money was slow in coming, even in the first year or two. The Upper Sioux claimed they received only half the sum promised them.

Dr. Mayo recalled the Indians had gathered at the Yellow Medicine agency for their May festival to celebrate the government's annual payment on ceded land. This year the agent had bad news for them.

Congress had voted no money. Congress was too immersed in the troubles of the Civil War to be concerned over the bickerings of a tribe of Indians in isolated Minnesota.

For weeks the Indians waited at the agency for money that didn't come. They grew fretful, then angry. Their anger heightened with the rising temperature of summer.

Their Great White Father in Washington had spurned them, they decided.

Until the white men came, the Indians had vast plains on which to grow their corn and forests in which to hunt game. Now their fields were restricted. The harvest of 1861 was a failure. The tribesmen had little to eat. The white men must help them.

And so, on the insistence of Little Crow, chief of the Lower Sioux, Joseph Galbraith, Indian Agent, summoned a council of traders and Indian chieftains to Fort Ridgely to talk over the problem.

They assembled August 15, the traders indifferent and scornful, the Indians tense and hostile. The Rev. Dr. Thomas S. Williamson, a Presbyterian missionary, was called in by the agent to serve as interpreter for the conference.

Facing Agent Galbraith, Chief Little Crow folded his arms slowly and looked long and searchingly into the white man's face. His heavy-featured countenance lacked expression, except for its habitual seriousness. Although shorter than some of the chieftains surrounding him, he seemed to tower above the coldness of his audience.

As he started to speak slowly, a breeze ruffled the feathers of his elaborate headdress. The tones came from deep within him, bearing a heavy sadness.

"We have waited a long time," he began. "The money is ours, but we cannot get it. We have no food, but here are your stores, filled with food. We ask that you, the agent, make some arrangement by which we can get food from the stores, or else we may take our own way to keep ourselves from starving. . . . When men are hungry, they help themselves!"

Little Crow turned abruptly and rejoined the ranks of his aids. Agent Galbraith looked at the traders, sitting impassively at his right.

"Well, Myrick, and you, La Bathe, what do you say?" he asked. "Will you extend them credit?"

The traders drew together for a whispered consultation. They talked briefly and then one, Francis La Bathe, stepped up to the agent.

"We will take our cue from Myrick," he said. "He is the only one of us who owns a share in the store he operates. Whatever Myrick does, we will do."

As soon as the missionary had interpreted La Bathe's comment, the burning eyes of the Indians focused on Andrew J. Myrick. The trader's gruff manner betrayed his resentment at being left to decide the council's fate. Anger swam in his eyes and it appeared for an instant that he would pour out the venom that bittered his tongue.

Instead, he turned without a word and started to walk from the meeting.

"Myrick! Myrick! What do you say?" Galbraith called after the departing trader.

Without pausing, Myrick snarled over his shoulder, "So far as I'm concerned, let them eat grass!"

The meaning of Myrick's parting thrust hardly needed
Dr. Williamson's interpretation. Its full purport struck the
Indians with staggering force. For a moment they were
silent, too numbed to protest.

Suddenly they sprang to their feet. The tense silence
was broken by echoing war whoops. Running to their horses
tethered outside the meeting place, they leaped to the ponies'
backs and vanished in the forest.

The Sioux were on their way to give Myrick his answer:
blood.

Having come to this Minnesota outpost as a humanitarian,
Dr. Mayo now found himself about to take an unexpected
role in a drama of human savagery. A pioneer in a land
where only the strong survived, he willingly joined his
neighbors in the battle thrust upon them.

America was the natural outlet for the personality of the
little English doctor, a warrior at heart and a politician
always. He had lived eventful years, and faced many more.
They were the outcome of the atmosphere of strife in which
he was born, on May 31, 1819.

It was the same month and year of Queen Victoria's
birth. The Napoleonic wars were over and England was
stirring as a mighty industrial nation. Food was scarce, however, and crowds of malcontents were protesting the ob-
noxious "corn laws." Factory workers especially were in
distress and the economic difficulties of England were largely
influential in causing young Mayo to emigrate to America.

His father was James Mayo, a former sea captain residing
near Manchester. He had some means and was able to give
William unusual educational advantages. William was tu-

tored in languages by a French refugee and later studied under John Dalton, founder of the atomic theory, while attending Owens College, the forerunner of the University of Manchester.

Early England had its quota of famous Mayos. One, who spelled his name John Mayow and lived between 1643 and 1679, was a physician and chemist of repute. Later a team of Mayos, Herbert and Thomas, served at Middlesex Hospital in London.

In 1845, when twenty-six years old, William Mayo joined the thousands of immigrants pouring into America. He came equipped with enough knowledge of chemistry and physics to obtain employment as an instructor in a New York hospital, which served as a medical school.

It was the era of the befogged medical practices of the Middle Ages. Surgery was a last resort in a desperate case. The patient was usually dying. Why not operate? It made little difference whether he succumbed a day sooner or later.

The surgeon probably sharpened his knife on the sole of his shoe and gripped it in his teeth while he adjusted a blood-stained apron over his business suit. The kitchen table in the patient's home served as the operating platform.

In those days, doctors put no stock in microbes. They blamed "bad air" for infections and had the windows nailed shut. Bloody incisions were mopped up with a common sponge and the surgeon washed up *after* the operation. Why before, when it was necessary to do a dirty job first?

The West, and its manifold opportunities, appealed to young Mayo. In 1847 he reached Lafayette, Indiana, and met Dr. Eleazar Deming, who conducted classes in medicine. Mayo became one of his most faithful pupils. When Dr. Deming left Indiana to become associated with McDowell's

Medical College at St. Louis, Missouri, Mayo followed to continue his studies.

From 1847 to 1857, McDowell's operated as the medical department of the University of Missouri. Mayo was graduated from the institution in 1854. The school was taken over by the Washington University in 1899.

Before going to St. Louis, Mayo paid court to a slim, cheerful girl who lived with her uncle in La Porte. She was Louise Abigail Wright, who had come west in a prairie schooner from her birthplace at Jordan, Onondaga County, New York. She had been born December 23, 1825.

On February 2, 1851, when Mayo was thirty-two and Louise twenty-six, they were married at La Porte. The bride was a gifted young woman, studious and intelligent. She was a worthy helpmate to the ambitious young medical student. Together they went to St. Louis to continue their education.

Medical schools mushroomed in all parts of the country in the middle nineteenth century, and Dr. Mayo was not one to let an opportunity escape him. After receiving his doctor's degree at St. Louis, he and his wife returned to Indiana and with Dr. William Heath Byford opened a medical school at La Porte. Fire destroyed the building and their equipment and brought a disastrous end to that venture.

Like many other newcomers, Mayo found Indiana's weather unfriendly. He suffered greatly from "fever and ague," commonly referred to as "the shakes." When he could no longer bear the distress it caused him, he decided to "ride it out" with team and buggy.

Kissing his wife and two babies, Gertrude and Phoebe, he set out in the summer of 1854 for the West, intending to return as soon as he was cured to resume his medical practice.

He drove through Chicago, then growing out of its lake swamp, and continued on to Galena, Illinois. There he was caught by the frenzy of eager emigrants, who told tall tales of wealth to be had at St. Paul and in the Lake Superior region. Moreover, the climate was ideal, Dr. Mayo was assured. "The shakes" didn't exist there and "consumption" was practically unknown.

At Dunleith, the river landing point twelve miles from Galena, Dr. Mayo watched the steamers load their cargoes of freight and passengers. The "fever of adventure" seized him. He made a quick and important decision.

Racing back to Indiana, he told Louise of the great country to the northwest that offered so much. The snow was hardly gone next spring before he packed his family, his surgical instruments and medical books into his buggy and set out once more for the Minnesota frontier.

After the tedious three-hundred-and-ninety-seven-mile journey up the Mississippi River in a jam-packed steamer early in 1855, the Mayos reached St. Paul, where every one of its ten thousand inhabitants was bent on a single mission—that of getting rich.

Speculation was the chief industry. Blood flowed almost as freely as whisky.

St. Paul was just beginning to live down its first epithet—Pig's Eye Landing, which did honor to a French-Canadian bootlegger, one Pierre Parrant, the first settler.

St. Paul escaped its porcine cognomen through the good offices of Father Pierre Galtier, who erected a log chapel at the townsite in 1841 and gave it the dignity of the apostle's name.

While he found need for his professional knowledge in St. Paul, Dr. Mayo decided the returns from his calling were meager indeed when compared to the possibilities the virgin northland afforded. He would become a copper prospector and hunt for the Superior range's fabulous mineral wealth. Obtaining employment from the Northwest Exploring Company, he set out into the wilderness, leaving his family in St. Paul. Mrs. Mayo opened a millinery shop to support herself and her children in her husband's absence, a practice she resorted to on other occasions before the doctor's income was sufficient to guarantee household necessities.

With a pack on his back, Dr. Mayo hiked the hundred miles along forest trails to Lake Superior to seek copper deposits. He found a promising spot and staked out a claim on property that now belongs to the United States Steel Company. Then he hired an Indian to guard it against claim jumpers.

Even in that remote region, Dr. Mayo found expression for his political leanings. The territorial governor, W. A. Gorman, named him chairman of the first board of county commissioners and in that capacity he selected the site of Duluth, Minnesota, as the seat of St. Louis county.

Dr. Mayo's pursuit of wealth ended ignominiously. When he returned to his copper exploring, he found his claim had been jumped. The purpose of his venture was now defeated and he decided to return to St. Paul.

One night, weary physically and low mentally, he built his campfire beside a small stream and settled in his blankets to sleep. A few hours later he awakened with a start. A pet spaniel, his only companion, was howling in alarm.

Dr. Mayo's campfire had burned out of control. His bedding and equipment were afire.

Throwing off the smoldering blanket, Dr. Mayo escaped serious burns. But he was helpless in a forest, without food, camping gear, and many miles from home. His only choice was to start walking southward.

For five days he tramped. He had nothing to eat; he met no one to help him. Almost exhausted, he was forced to kill the pet dog that had saved his life and prepare a distasteful meal.

His strength partly restored, he plodded on until he reached the St. Croix River. There he came upon a half-breed Indian who possessed a canoe. With the Indian he paddled down the St. Croix to Stillwater, from where he walked the remaining twenty miles to St. Paul.

Although he had almost fallen victim to the unfriendly northland, Dr. Mayo was neither dismayed nor discouraged. When he saw medicine would not pay in St. Paul, he did not hesitate to put his family aboard a Minnesota River flatboat and set out for St. Peter to become a farmer.

Prospecting, surveying, farming, steamboating—none was for the little doctor. Medicine was his forte. But before the name Mayo was to mean much in Minnesota or anywhere else, the doctor was called to battle the Indians in the bloody uprising of 1862.

CHAPTER THREE

Dr. Mayo Called to War

OUR HUNGRY SIOUX INDIANS, returning from an unsuccessful hunt in the Big Woods of Eastern Minnesota, came to a rail fence bordering Robinson Jones' farm near Acton in Meeker County. It was a fateful Sunday—August 17, 1862—and the four braves, Brown Wing, Breaking Up, Killing Ghost, and Runs Against Something When Crawling, discovered a fateful nest of eggs hidden in the grass. Killing Ghost started to pick them up.

"Don't take them," Brown Wing admonished. "They are white man's eggs. You will get into trouble."

Killing Ghost's anger overcame his hunger. Dashing the eggs to the ground, he sneered at Brown Wing. "You are a coward. You are afraid of the white man, even though you are half starved. I will tell everyone you are a coward."

"I am not a coward," Brown Wing said. "I am afraid of no white man. To show you, I will go to the house and shoot him. Are you brave enough to go with me?"

"Yes, I will go with you and we will see who is the braver."

Runs Against Something When Crawling and Breaking Up, not to be outdone, said, "We will go with you and we will be brave, too."

Robinson Jones and his wife, alarmed by the Indians approaching their home so stealthily, fled to the near-by home of Howard Baker, a son-in-law, where several persons had gathered for a Sunday visit. The Sioux ran after the settlers and dashed into the Baker dwelling, firing as they entered. Before the whites could make a defense, the Indians had slain Jones and his wife, Howard Baker, his daughter, Martha, fourteen years old, and a visitor, Judd Webster. Then stealing Baker's team of horses, the braves drove to Chief Shakopee's camp six miles above the Redwood agency.

Although it was night when they arrived at the Indian village, they aroused all who would listen to their story of bravery. Excitement swept the camp. Chief Shakopee started off with the four slayers to report to Chief Little Crow, his superior, who lived two miles from the agency. Little Crow sat up in bed to hear the account of the murders.

"War is now declared," Little Crow said grimly. "The payments on our lands will stop. There will be bloodshed. The whites will take a dreadful revenge."

The band was called into council. Chiefs Wabasha, Wacouta, and Big Eagle argued for peace, but few would listen. The cry: "Kill the whites!" resounded through the village. The council voted war against the white settlers.

Into the placid Minnesota River valley soon after rode

seven thousand Sioux, seeking revenge against an alien horde that had usurped their lands, their streams, their hunting grounds.

They brandished arms, shot ammunition, and rode horses either stolen from or supplied by the white traders. Traders who often cheated them . . . traders who now refused to give them food against the day when they could harvest a good crop and pay their debts.

Hunger had driven them out of control.

Led by Little Crow, the warriors plunged the countryside into a blood-and-fire bath. Up and down the valley settlers fled from burning homes and fields, leaving behind mutilated bodies of friends and families. The living sped desperately to any settlement that promised refuge; the dead paid the price of the white man's advancing civilization.

Panic stalked across the land from Dakota to St. Paul. Death and destruction, hatred and revenge—all this, because a keg of gold was a few hours late in delivery. The Minnesota Indian massacres of 1862 are recorded on such a thin margin of time. History has few more ironic episodes.

After the Sioux had waited in vain at the Yellow Medicine agency in May for their land payments, Congress finally made a delayed appropriation. A keg of gold, enough to meet the redmen's claims, reached St. Paul on August 16 by river steamer.

Next day it was dispatched to Fort Ridgely, where it arrived at midday on the eighteenth. But Little Crow and his tribesmen knew nothing about it. They had, some hours before, received and accepted Myrick's answer to their appeal for credit: "Let them eat grass!"

Little Crow did not wait long to give poetic reply to the trader's ultimatum. Andrew J. Myrick was one of the first settlers slain by the war-mad Indians. His mouth was stuffed with grass.

Proceeding like a military strategist, Little Crow directed his warriors at Fort Ridgely and the territory around it. New Ulm, a German community of twelve hundred inhabitants, was almost in sight of the fort. The Indian chief was confident that once he had wiped out the guard at Ridgely, his battle was won. The fort was the door to the valley that opened the way to St. Paul, at the junction of the Minnesota and Mississippi rivers. Once through that door, the Indians could sweep beyond, unchecked until they reached the Father of Waters.

New Ulm was, of all the Minnesota frontier towns, the most exposed to Indian attack. Situated on a prairie a mile from the river, it afforded little protection against the cunning maneuvers of the swift-striking redmen.

Charging with such suddenness that New Ulm was caught unprepared, a raiding party of Dakota braves gave the first warning that the Indians were determined to sweep the valley clear of towns and farms alike. The attack came in midafternoon. After a charge that drove the citizens to cover in houses and outbuildings at the edge of town, the Indians settled down to sniping. For an hour and a half they held the town in a state of terror.

Then Providence took a hand. A sudden rainstorm rolled out of the southwest. Great black clouds cast a dusklike pall over the battleground. The shower broke with as much fury as the attacking redmen. Quickly the gunfire ceased as the elements commanded the battle. When the storm passed half an hour later, the Indians had vanished. Not a single body remained behind to indicate the toll of the white sharpshooters. Only the bullet-marked homes and here and there a wounded white man, writhing on the rain-soaked ground, bore witness to the clash. Leaving the injured in the care of several women, the defenders gathered to discuss their plight.

"We've got to have assistance immediately," they agreed. "This attack is just a taste of what's to come. We're exposed to the full fury of Little Crow's rascals."

"How are we going to get it?" a grim townsman asked. "It's worth your life to leave the village. Those Indians are probably waiting for any move we make to send word outside."

"Of course they are. But someone must take the chance. We've got to get word to Judge Flandrau at Traverse de Sioux, first of all. He'll raise a company of volunteers from St. Peter and Le Sueur and help us defend New Ulm."

"Who'll go?"

"We need a young fellow who isn't afraid of anything. How about you, Rudolph?"

A tanned lad of seventeen, his face streaked with powder smoke and his eyes aglow with excitement, pushed into the circle of men. Rudolph Schultz had matured to manhood in that brief battle with the Indians. He was ready for any duty to save his people.

"Sure, let me go," he insisted. "If I can have Todd Archer's pony, I'll get through."

"The horse is yours," Archer called from the fringe of the crowd. "He's the fastest animal in the valley, and with a fifty-yard start there isn't an Indian that can catch you."

The pony was hustled over from a near-by stable. Rudolph swung lightly to its bare back. He waited impatiently for last instructions.

"You've got a fifteen-mile ride to Judge Flandrau's place,"

he was told, "so you've got to make fast time. The judge will know what to do as soon as he hears about the attack. Now, be careful! Take the trail down to the grove at the river, then hit out across the prairie, just as fast as your horse can leg. You'll outrun the Indians if you get into the clear."

With a wave of his arm, Rudolph Schultz sped from New Ulm toward the waiting warriors.

Dusk was deepening into a starless night when Judge Charles E. Flandrau settled himself before his stone fireplace in his home at Traverse de Sioux. There was a sting to the early fall air that the gay birch flame dissipated quickly. The bright glow from the hearthstones illumined the judge's gray face and revealed lines of worry. As he slowly lighted his pipe, he thought of the disquieting reports from the agency and the Army post. Surely the days of Indian outbreaks could not come again, he told himself. He forced himself to settle back in his huge chair to relax.

Horse's hoofs, pounding furiously along his drive, startled him. He pushed himself from his chair and strode to the front door. Just as he opened it, a young horseman on a lather-streaked pony drew rein in front of him. For several seconds horse and rider were hidden in a fog of dust.

"Hello out there!" Flandrau called. "Who is it? What's the confounded hurry?"

Breathless from excitement and his frenzied ride, Rudolph Schultz gasped, "The Sioux . . . they've . . . they're on the warpath. They've attacked New Ulm, sir—this afternoon. We're afraid they're coming back. We need help—right away."

"Indians attacking New Ulm! So it's come. Just what I was afraid of." Judge Flandrau snatched his coat from a chair and dashed outside. Running toward the stable he called,

"George . . . Carl, where are you?" His hired hands stood silhouetted in the square of light that marked the barn door.

"George, get on your horse and ride . . . ride to St. Peter. Tell every man you see to report to me at once. The Indians are attacking New Ulm."

"Indians?"

"Don't ask questions! Carl, you ride for Le Sueur. You get Dr. Mayo and bring him back here. Don't let anything stop you. And you"—the judge turned to the tired lad behind him—"ride out that way and . . ."

For the first time Flandrau noticed the fatigue of the youngster who had fought Indians in the afternoon and had been dodging them since. "No," he said. "Go into the house and tell the cook to give you supper. I'll ride out myself."

Saddling his own horse, he mounted and sped away.

Carl Mystrum had already vanished in the darkness. Judge Flandrau's hired hand was whipping his stout pony on a thirty-mile ride to bring Dr. Mayo to the aid of New Ulm's victims of the marauding redmen.

CHAPTER FOUR

Doctor Turns Indian Fighter

A WEARY MAN MOANED IN HIS sleep and turned restlessly. Beside him his half-awakened wife wondered whether the Carlton baby that had kept the doctor out so late was a boy or a girl.

She decided to wait until morning to ask and settled back on her pillow. She was nearly asleep again when the beat of a horse galloping along the road startled her. The thud of hoofs on hard ground grew louder.

Sitting up, she could just see out the front window. There, in the fading dimness of night, she saw a rider dismount and scurry up the front walk. Immediately there followed the impatient clatter of the door knocker.

"Will! Will! Wake up! There's someone at the door." Louise Mayo touched her husband at the shoulder and shook him gently. "I suppose it's another baby," she told herself, sharing the weariness that numbed the doctor.

Mumbling in his sleep, Dr. Mayo turned on his side and drew the bedcovers tighter under his chin.

Again the door knocker sent a shiver of sound through the house. It was followed by a commanding hail: "Dr. Mayo! Dr. Mayo!"

Grasping the blanket, Louise pulled it away and shook the doctor once more. "Will! Will! You must get up. Someone outside is calling you."

"Huh? What's that?" The sleepy physician raised himself on an elbow. Again the stranger shouted, this time his impatient voice tensed with alarm.

Dr. Mayo swung briskly from bed and fumbled on the dark floor until he found his slippers. He shuffled across the room and pulled wide the window.

"What's the trouble with you out there?" he called. "What do you want with me at this hour?"

"Indians!"

"Indians? What Indians? Where?"

"They've attacked New Ulm. This—yesterday afternoon. Judge Flandrau sent me for you. He's calling for volunteers to help defend the town. He wants you, especially. Told me I had to bring you back. Every man that Le Sueur can spare is needed at New Ulm."

Louise joined her husband at the window. She was trembling. "Will, tell him not to awaken the children. Tell him I'll be right down to let him in."

She hurried away, turning first to the crib where her year-old son, Will, slept undisturbed. Then she looked into the bedroom where Gertrude and Phoebe lay side by side. Satisfied they had not heard, she sped downstairs.

Dr. Mayo, through long practice, dressed quickly in the dark. He grabbed his medicine kit from the bedside table and followed Louise. He found the horseman standing impatiently in the kitchen, where Mrs. Mayo was lighting the stove.

"I'm Carl Mystrum," the visitor explained. "I work for Flandrau. Some of the men have been wounded in the fighting at New Ulm. He said to be sure you came."

"Of course," Dr. Mayo said. "If you'll go out to the stable and saddle my pony, the bay one, I'll be with you in a few minutes."

Carl left immediately. Dr. Mayo rummaged in the kitchen closet for his musket. When he looked out into the yard he saw by the first trace of dawn that Carl was already leading his horse toward the house.

Bending over Louise, busy mixing a batter of wheat cakes, Dr. Mayo kissed her warmly and started out the door.

"Will, you can't leave without breakfast!" Louise cried. "Call that man in. I'll have something for you in a few minutes."

"No, no. There isn't time for that. Indians are on the warpath, people wounded. We can't stop for breakfast." He was in the saddle by the time he had finished talking.

"You must have a cup of coffee, at least," Louise called from the doorway. In an instant she reappeared carrying a steaming cup in each hand.

"Now, don't become alarmed—keep the children in the house—you, too— Whew, that coffee's hot—and good." He perforated his instructions with gulps of the beverage. "We'll stop those redmen before they get this far. Got to. Don't worry—I'll be home in a day or two."

Returning the cup to Louise, whose sensitive face betrayed

the fear and anxiety she felt, Dr. Mayo followed Carl down the trail toward Traverse de Sioux, just west of St. Peter.

Dusk again was chasing the sun from the reddening sky when the two saddle-weary men reined in at Flandrau's farmstead. They found some hundred-odd men gathered in groups, talking, speculating, waiting nervously to be on their way. Each carried a rifle or a musket. Dr. Mayo reported immediately to the judge, a tall, spare man marked by a commanding dignity unusual among the rough characters of the region.

"Hello, Doctor. I'm indeed glad you got here so quickly," Judge Flandrau said. "We are about to head out for New Ulm. Hope you're not too tired."

"Oh no, Judge. I'm used to a lot of riding. How are things around here? Seen any more of the Indians?"

"They're still around, all right, but apparently it's Chief Big Eagle's band waiting for the main pack under Little Crow to arrive from up the valley. Scouts say they're moving in fast. That's why we've got to reach New Ulm as quickly as we can."

"How many men have you here?"

"About a hundred, all from downriver. A few more may show up later, but we can't wait longer. We had a meeting a bit ago and the men wanted me to take command as captain. Is that suitable to you, Doctor?"

"Indeed it is. You give the orders and we'll carry them out."

"Fine. All right, men!" he called in a deep voice. "We'll start at once for New Ulm. Stick close together, guns ready. No talking. I don't think we'll be molested. Ready! Forward!"

The morning of August 23 dawned chill and foreboding.

For hours New Ulm's two hundred tensed defenders, augmented by Flandrau's "Frontier Guard," had waited for the expected attack.

Little Crow had arrived to join forces with Chief Big Eagle. With a thousand well-armed and mounted warriors, thirsty for more blood after their successful raids down the valley, they waited just beyond eye range, ready for battle. Scouts had warned in the night that the tribesmen would begin their assault on the town with daylight.

Dr. Mayo, his musket beside him and his medicine kit pushed under a log, lay behind a felled tree. Carl Mystrum was at his left and a neighbor from Le Sueur at his right.

"They're a thousand against us, but don't let that shake you," Dr. Mayo warned. "Shoot straighter than they do, and save your bullets. Just don't get rattled. . . ."

"Here they come!" A lookout, hidden high in the cupola of a near-by barn, shouted the warning.

Over the horizon ballooned a cloud of yellow dust that grew larger and larger in the morning haze. Then the stillness was broken by the whoops of a thousand blood-mad warriors. The thunder of horses' hoofs, pounding hollowly on the prairie, drummed in the ears of the waiting whitemen.

Like a brown avalanche, the Indians slid across the open field. Just as it appeared that they would engulf the town, the defenders met them with a blast of gunfire, full into the charging mass. The first volley pitched a dozen braves from their mounts. Horses stumbled and fell, rolled across prostrate bodies. Screams, the crash of rifles, defiant war cries brought an end to the clear day's sanity.

Magically, taut nerves became calm. The awful waiting was ended. In action the riflemen relaxed. Coolly, deliberately, they picked off an Indian here, a pony there, cutting down the yelling pack.

Dr. Mayo fired half a dozen shots into the deluge of howling redmen. He watched them break, re-form a solid front, and charge again. Once more the savages were beaten off, only to circle and attack from another quarter.

A faint moan caught Dr. Mayo's attention. He turned. Carl Mystrum lay prostrate, his face pressed to the ground. A streak of crimson marked the path of an Indian's bullet across his cheek. A splotch of red, widening slowly, revealed where the lead had buried itself in Carl's shoulder.

Dropping his musket, Dr. Mayo knelt beside the wounded man. He pulled his medicine kit from beneath the log. Quickly tearing away the blood-soaked shirt, he sponged the wound and applied a stout bandage. In a minute he stanched the ragged hole.

"Ed! Ed!" he called. "Give me a lift, Carl's been hit. We've got to get him into town to take better care of him."

Dr. Mayo didn't raise his gun again to fight Little Crow's Indians. In a few minutes cries of "Dr. Mayo, over here!" and "Dr. Mayo! Help! This way!" kept the little doctor racing from one injured man to another. He had all he could do, and more, to patch the holes torn in legs, arms, and stomachs by the revengeful warriors.

The morning wore on, with the Indians pressing in with unabated determination. The New Ulm defenders were barely holding their own. Already thirteen of them lay dead. Nearly two score injured filled beds and cots the women had set up in the community hall.

"Flandrau, it's becoming critical," Dr. Mayo said when he met the volunteers' commander at noon. "We need more men. We'll be in a desperate position if this fight turns into a siege."

"You're right, Doctor, but right now we can't do a thing except keep on fighting. If we get any help, it's got to come from the settlements down the river. How they are going to get past that heathen pack out there is more than I can say."

"Little Crow certainly picked our worst time to rebel. He knew the regulars are in training at Snelling for Civil War duty. Troops couldn't get down here for days. Unless more volunteers arrive soon, we're not going to fight off the tribe much longer."

The two men were interrupted by a grizzled scout running toward them. His face heralded exciting news.

"Judge Flandrau!" he called when still some distance away. "There's a party of horsemen back on the plain ready to come through and help us. But it looks like they're afraid to move closer."

Mayo and Flandrau gazed to the west. On a distant elevation fifty or more horsemen, garbed in the typical dress of frontiersmen, milled about uncertainly.

"Judge, they're waiting for us to open the way," Dr. Mayo said. "Let me call for volunteers for a sortie. I'm sure we can get enough to open a path through the attackers."

"Jove, we've got to do it. Go ahead, Mayo. It's a godsend."

"Men of New Ulm!" Dr. Mayo shouted after mounting a store platform in sight of numerous riflemen. "There's a party of horsemen across the plain, waiting a chance to come to our rescue. It's too dangerous for them to move in while the Indians block the way. We've got to drive back the savages and let the reinforcements reach us. Who will volunteer to take part in the sortie?"

"Here's one!"

"I'll go."

"So will I."

A score of eager men ran forward. Captain W. W. Dodd, second in command, stepped up. His calmness spread confidence in those about him. "I'll take charge of the party if you wish, Judge."

"Thank you, Dodd. You're the very man I want."

Quickly the men were mounted and equipped with fresh rifles and ammunition. Charging down the street, they headed across the plain toward the waiting horsemen. The Indians fell back, keeping well out of range of the sortie.

Mayo and Flandrau, standing together to watch Captain Dodd's mission, were startled to see the horsemen pull up suddenly when a little distance from the waiting troop.

At that instant the "rescuers" charged toward Dodd's men, firing as they rode.

"My God, Flandrau, it's a trap!" Dr. Mayo gasped. "They're Indians, disguised as whites!"

"They've tricked us, Mayo! Those wily rascals have dressed themselves in clothes stolen from raided farmhouses. I should have expected that!"

Fleeing desperately, the betrayed defenders stormed into the village, pursued by the warriors. A crashing volley from the town riflemen turned them aside once more and saved the returning horsemen. A quick count revealed that half a dozen men, including Captain Dodd, had been slain.

"Well, Mayo, it looks more than ever like a hard, long fight," Flandrau said, shaking his head over Dodd's disastrous ride. "We can't take any more chances with our men. Everyone must keep under cover. We'll wait out Little Crow and his pack if it takes until winter."

As the day waned, the Indians withdrew far beyond gun range to rest their horses and care for their wounded. Occasionally a horseman would dash forward and shoot a flaming arrow at an exposed building.

The respite gave the New Ulm defenders an opportunity to check their losses and resources. Dr. Mayo welcomed the breathing spell to give closer attention to the injured fighters. But it also gave him a chance to reflect not only on New Ulm's plight, but upon his own family's peril at Le Sueur.

The Indian outbreak had suddenly become far more distressing than he believed would prove likely. Troops ordinarily stationed at Fort Ridgely were away preparing for Civil War duty. The Indians far outnumbered the able-bodied whites. At first they had butchered farmers and settlers in isolated homes. Now they were concentrating on the valley towns. Should New Ulm fall, there was little hope but that St. Peter, Mankato, and then Le Sueur would go down likewise, with an appalling slaughter.

Le Sueur, and with it his family, was defenseless now that practically every man able to fight had joined Flandrau's "Frontier Guard." Other heads of families faced the same quandary and shared Dr. Mayo's worries. They could fight only the harder at New Ulm to stop the redmen at the gateway to the valley.

Dr. Mayo's thoughts about Louise and his three children would have been lightened immeasurably could he have observed the drama in wit and bravery enacted by his wife and the other women of Le Sueur.

The day following the departure of the volunteers to New Ulm's defense, a band of Indians on horseback was discovered spying on the town from a near-by height.

Mrs. Wilkins, a neighbor, ran into the Mayo kitchen, incoherent with terror.

"Oh, Mrs. Mayo, Mrs. Mayo!" she wailed. "Oh dear, oh dear, Mrs. Mayo!"

"What's the matter, Mrs. Wilkins? Calm yourself!"

"Oh, Mrs. Mayo! Indians! Indians! Oh, Mrs. Mayo, what'll we *do?*"

The doctor's wife peered out of her kitchen door cautiously. She saw nothing. Going into the yard, she glanced over the horizon. She observed the tribesmen outlined against the blue sky.

Panic rose in her breast and she fought to conquer it. Then an idea crowded out her fears. If she could only get the women of the village . . .

"Gertrude . . . Phoebe, where are you?"

The children came running from the front lawn. "Here, Mother."

"Run, tell all the women you see to come here immediately. Everyone you can find."

"But, Mother, why?"

"Don't ask questions. Do as I tell you. Hurry! Mrs. Wilkins, you run too. Bring back every woman you can reach in the village. Don't explain anything. Just tell them they must come here at once."

While her messengers sped away, Mrs. Mayo hurried to a clothes closet and donned a pair of her husband's trousers and a suit coat. She found an old felt hat and crushed it over her hair.

Then she ran to the stable and hunted until she found a hayfork. By the time she returned to the house, several women, trembling with fear and excitement, stood in the yard. Their bewilderment made them helpless.

"Oh, Mrs. Mayo, we'll be massacred. . . ."

"Please be quiet. This is no time to lose your head. Do as I tell you and the Indians won't bother us. I want all of you to put on your men's clothes—overalls, coats, pants, anything you can find, just as I have. Then come back with rifles, if you have any. Otherwise bring hoes, rakes, sticks with knives tied to them—anything that will look like a gun.

"Now, don't do a lot of talking. Just keep yourself calm and do as I tell you. Hurry now and be back as quickly as you can."

As soon as the other women reported, Mrs. Mayo gave them similar instructions. In less than half an hour, more than fifty women, looking like an ill-fitted tramp army, assembled in the Mayo yard.

"Now, women of Le Sueur, we will line up, two by two, and march into the village," Mrs. Mayo said. "At the square, we'll go through whatever maneuvers we can to represent a company drilling. If we do this seriously, I'm certain the Indians will not attack. Forward, march!"

Led by the little doctor's wife, the feminine warriors, armed with as mute a collection of firearms as a troop of infantry ever shouldered, marched down the dusty road to the village square.

The Indians on the near-by heights watched restlessly.

CHAPTER FIVE

The Mayo Skeleton

THE SIEGE OF NEW ULM WAS late in its second day. Little Crow had driven his warriors at the town repeatedly, only to have the whites turn them back with deadly marksmanship.

Flaming arrows, burrowing into the parched roofs of the town, fired scores of dwellings and barns. Charred timbers and smoke-stained stone walls gave evidence of the ruin that was slowly reducing the community to an untenable outpost. Twenty-nine men who had fought New Ulm's fight had been killed. Many more lay wounded. Smoke from half a dozen burning dwellings drifted across the flat field before the town. It concealed for a time the Sioux braves, now wary of the sharpshooting defenders.

At dusk the last red horseman dropped from sight. Watch-

43

ing every Indian maneuver for some new trap, Judge Flandrau took advantage of the respite to call his men together after posting several as lookouts.

"Defenders of New Ulm," he began. "I believe the time has come to abandon the community. The Indians have withdrawn, probably to await reinforcements and then attack with new fury and cunning. We dare not expose the women and children longer to the possibility of a massacre. I propose that as soon as darkness comes we move New Ulm's twelve hundred inhabitants to Mankato."

"That's a tremendous task, Judge," Dr. Mayo interrupted. "Have we enough wagons for the journey?"

"Perhaps one of you New Ulm freighters can tell us. How about it, someone?"

"There's probably a hundred and fifty rigs hereabouts," a bearded teamster volunteered. "They should be enough to haul the whole town."

"They've got to be," Flandrau replied. "We must cover the twenty-five miles to Mankato as fast as possible. We've got to travel light. Spread the word. Get the women and children together first. Load food and water in each wagon, but little else. We'll start just as soon as it's dark. Guards will ride in the van, at the sides and in the rear. In case of attack, the leaders will circle the train and we'll all fight . . . fight to the end."

"There's not a minute to waste," Dr. Mayo added. "Come on, some of you men. We've got to get the wounded in the strongest wagons. And you women. Bring all your bedding. It's a rough ride and those fellows carrying lead will need more than boards under them to take the jolts."

That night a creaking train of one hundred and fifty-three wagons abandoned the battle-scarred town of New Ulm, leaving behind nearly two hundred burned dwellings. Stopping only briefly to rest their oxen and horses, the refugees kept well ahead of the roving Indian bands. They reached Mankato safely next day.

"What's the news from Le Sueur?" Dr. Mayo asked the first Mankato citizen he recognized. "Any trouble down the river?"

"Say, that woman of yours, she's a good one," the Mankatoan said. "She put pants on the women up there and scared all the Indians away. She's a good one, she is."

"I don't know what you mean, sir," Dr. Mayo said with some warmth. "What happened?"

Dr. Mayo heard the story of the Le Sueur coup. The Indians had watched the feminine company march around the village square several times and decided the place was too well guarded to attack. They were careful to avoid it thereafter.

Mrs. Mayo suddenly became the heroine of the uprising. Her stanchness and bravery gave courage to every settler who heard the tale. Dr. Mayo, freed from his duties of caring for New Ulm's wounded, hurried home, a proud and happy husband.

The evacuation of New Ulm and the continued assaults of the tribesmen on exposed areas finally brought action from the Federal government. Troops taken from Fort Ridgely and other posts for Civil War training were dispatched into the Minnesota River valley again.

On September 23, the Army cornered Little Crow's band at Wood Lake, and in the resultant battle the Sioux power was smashed. The Indians were holding two hundred and sixty-nine white prisoners, all of whom were rescued and turned over to General Henry Hastings Sibley.

The uprising, despite its brevity, took a tremendous toll from the Minnesota frontier. Six hundred and forty-four citizens were massacred, ninety-three soldiers lost their lives in battle, and uncounted hundreds of settlers wounded in clashes with the redmen.

Property damage was estimated to run well over two million dollars. The tribesmen had exacted a bitter price before relinquishing forever their lands and streams. The Indian losses were not ascertained. Their dead and wounded were never left on the battlefield to be counted.

After the final battle, the Army held four hundred and twenty-five Indians captive. All went to trial before a military commission on charges of rebellion and murder. Three hundred and twenty-one were found guilty and sentenced to die.

When the East received the news that the rebellious Sioux faced execution, a cry arose against the persecution of the Indians. Pressure was applied at Washington and their case carried to President Lincoln.

Lincoln, although overburdened with problems of the Civil War, took time to consider the Indians' plight. He decreed that only thirty-eight should be hanged. Later he pardoned the others.

Christmas Day found hundreds of residents of the now peaceful Minnesota River valley moving on Mankato. They were bent on witnessing the last chapter in the Indian uprising of 1862. On the morrow, December 26, thirty-eight Indians were to hang for their crimes against the white settlers.

The trials had brought out the naïveté of the Sioux warriors. All pleaded innocent to the charges against them. If one stole a horse, it was a little horse, he insisted. If another fired a gun, it was an old gun and didn't shoot straight. If a third killed a settler, it was because the settler killed one of the Indian's brothers.

Chief Big Eagle paid the tribesmen's last tribute to their white enemies. "We thought Fort Ridgely was the door to the valley as far as to St. Paul," he testified, "and that if we got through the door, nothing could stop us this side of the Mississippi. But the defenders of the fort were very brave and kept the door shut." The state of Minnesota some years later presented to those brave defenders bronze medals which bore the Indian motto, "Ti-yo-pa Ma-ta-ka-pi" (They kept the door shut).

Dr. Mayo was among the several thousand citizens of the valley who gathered in Mankato that cold morning of December 26. A common scaffold, ugly and sinister, decorated the town square. Before it a regiment of troops was drawn. Behind the soldiers crowded men, women, and children in holiday mood.

The front door of the near-by jail opened. Two soldiers, rifles nestling under their arms, stepped out. Behind them walked single file the thirty-eight doomed Sioux, their hands tied behind their backs. Their appearance was greeted by a roar from the citizen throng, a cheer of triumph. Unheeding, the Indians trudged to the scaffold and climbed the steps slowly, chanting a death hymn.

Quickly several executioners slipped nooses over the heads of the Indians. Dr. Mayo, watching from behind the soldiers, recognized the sullen features of an old acquaintance—Cut Nose, the Sioux who had tried to steal his horse at the river ford. Cut Nose was described at the trial as "the most repulsive of the prisoners." He had leaped into a wagon loaded with women and children fleeing from an attacking Indian band and slain eleven.

As though on signal, the crowd grew tense and silent. The prisoners ceased their death chant. They protested their innocence once more. The white man was doing them an irreparable wrong. The white man was guilty. . . .

The trap was sprung. A row of bodies dangled at the end of thirty-eight strands of rope. Thirty-eight Sioux paid the penalty for their own and their brothers' crimes. As soon as the executions were completed, the corpses were cut down. Tossed into waiting wagons, they were hauled to the Minnesota River. On a sandbar, where a trench had been dug several hours before, the dead braves were unloaded and unceremoniously buried.

The crowd and the troops dispersed. The final page in a dark chapter of Minnesota history had been inscribed. But for Dr. Mayo and the Mayo brothers, one yet unborn, that last chapter opened a strange passage in medical lore. That passage concerns the "Skeleton of the Mayos."

It was nearly dusk when a short, energetic man walked across the frozen sands of the Minnesota River before Mankato. He stopped beside the trench where the thirty-eight Indian murderers lay buried. He thrust a spade into the freezing ground. He dug untiringly until he uncovered what he hunted, a certain body. He rolled the frozen corpse to the top of the trench and wrapped it in a blanket. Then, half-dragging and half-carrying it, he moved it to his waiting wagon.

Dr. William Worrall Mayo was not one to let the executions close an era without giving something of worth to a new one. He claimed that Indian body, the body of Cut

Nose, to teach him and his heirs new truths about human anatomy. When he reached home, he carefully dissected it and articulated the skeleton. That bony frame became the ever-handy skeleton in the Mayo closet. On long winter evenings, when father and sons spent hours together in common study, they paid many visits to the remains of Cut Nose to learn more about the functions of the bones and the mechanics of the human frame.

With the end of the Indian uprisings, the fortunes of the Mayo family took another eventful turn. The Civil War was again uppermost in the minds of all. The Federal government divided Minnesota into two recruiting districts and named Rochester headquarters of the southern area.

In 1855, Rochester was little more than a stagecoach station of a few shacks in the underbrush of the Zumbro River. By 1863 it had fifteen hundred inhabitants and was taking on the aspect of a boom town. Caravans of prairie schooners rolled through to the West, but many homestead seekers got no farther than the future Southern Minnesota metropolis.

Wheat ruled the town, where pioneer businessmen were seized with "Rochester emigration fever." Completion of the twenty-five-mile branch railroad from Winona, on the Mississippi, to Rochester was promised for 1864. When that event took place, Rochester's future was assured, everyone agreed. Shows and showmen found the lively farming community a paradise. Paradoxically, it early gave promise of a center for the practice of medicine. Many an Easterner fell victim to the aches, pains, and accidents of the westward migration. They overexerted, they were overexposed to adverse weather, they suffered from poor sanitation and careless hygiene. Rochester became the "end of the line" for a share of the migrants and they settled there to make the community a flourishing district capital, both social and economical.

It was to such a town that Dr. Mayo was transferred as examining surgeon. Under Captain Charles H. See of Caledonia, the provost marshal, the recruiting station was set up in Rochester to be nearer the railroad than was Le Sueur. Dr. Mayo was happy to make his abode in a new section of the state. His days at Le Sueur had been difficult ones at best, and Rochester offered considerably more to the professional man, despite the influx of quack doctors and charlatans who peddled their patent medicines to the suffering.

The shift was Le Sueur's loss and the eventual making of Rochester as one of the great medical centers of the world. Thomas Smullen, who lived next door the Mayos at Le Sueur, years later expressed the village's feeling over the departure of its famed resident.

"The Old Man was a good doctor in those days," Mr. Smullen recalled. "He was a mighty smart man on a number of subjects. He certainly did a great thing for Rochester when he moved there. He made that town, he and the boys. We wish he'd stayed in Le Sueur. We'd be world famous now, instead of Rochester."

It was a cold, damp day in the spring of 1863 when the Mayos reached Rochester after a cross-country drive from Le Sueur. Louise Mayo held her infant son, William, in a bundle of blankets while she scanned the rows of dwellings for one that might house her growing brood. The girls, Gertrude and Phoebe, peered from beneath a buffalo robe, wide-eyed but silent.

"It's a pretty place," Louise said finally. "How busy the

streets appear! Rochester must be a thriving community."

"It surely is, Louise. I think it is going to be one of the chief cities of the state someday, perhaps the first. When we get the railroad here, there's no telling how far we'll go."

"It should be an excellent place in which to build a good medical practice."

"Indeed. I've been told some physicians here have as many as a dozen patients a day. There may be a new field for us. The Indian war was hard on a good many persons, but it gave me experience in surgery I could never have had otherwise. It has given me new confidence in myself and in my ability as a surgeon."

Enthusiastic as he was over his change of residence, Dr. Mayo came to Rochester unheralded and with no special welcome, except for the universal cordiality extended to every new settler. The town neither knew or cared about a man's past. Dr. Mayo was just another doctor, albeit the examining surgeon for the provost marshal.

But William Worrall Mayo was to prove himself much greater than "just another doctor" coming to Rochester on the promptings of chance. He had battled his way through successive stages of failure. Now he was entering Rochester as full of enthusiasm and determination as he was the day he stepped ashore from the ocean vessel that brought him to New York.

In Rochester the Mayo fortunes were to take root. Until 1863, Dr. Mayo had hunted the lodestone of success. Thereafter, there was no longer need to press the search. The Mayo art of ministering to human ailments had found a broad and fresh canvas, one that the world would come to see.

CHAPTER SIX

Those Mayo Boys

HEN HIS DUTIES AS EXAMIN-
ing surgeon for the Army ended with the close of the Civil
War, Dr. Mayo had no worries about his future practice.
Rochester was home. As soon as he had his own office, he
built an old-fashioned angular house, ornamented in the
architecture of that period, on the site of the present Clinic
building.

Dr. W. A. Hyde, a newcomer in Rochester, who had
served in the Union Army, proposed to Dr. Mayo that they
enter business together. Dr. Mayo agreed.

They advertised their enterprise in the *Rochester City
Post* in 1864 thus:

"W. A. Hyde and W. W. Mayo, physicians and surgeons,

having formed a co-partnership for the practice of medicine and surgery, solicit a share of patronage. All calls answered. Office over Union Drugstore."

The partnership was unsatisfactory and it was dissolved after six months. Thereafter Dr. Mayo had only three permanent partners in medicine—his wife and his two sons—and this association was severed only in death.

Dr. Mayo's first son, William, was four years old when his second arrived to fill his role in medicine's greatest team of brothers. Charles Horace was born July 19, 1865. It was the year in which Sir Joseph Lister announced the success of his "carbolic spray," presaging antiseptic surgery. Compound fractures, at that time, almost always necessitated amputation, since no way had yet been discovered to control the infection.

A year after Charles's birth, the clinical thermometer first came into use. It was an awkward instrument, ten inches long, and required five minutes for a temperature reading.

Another advance in medicine came three years later when the wooden stethoscope was introduced. Physicians quickly found it a great help to them. It was a cumbersome instrument, but it fit snugly in the plug hats which distinguished doctors from laymen.

Louis Pasteur, along with Lister, was then centering his attention on germs, infection, and antisepsis. Medicine was growing up. And Dr. Mayo, although now past fifty, determined to grow up with it.

His practice at Rochester was typical of the country doctor of that day. His life was a hard one, requiring him to ride endless miles on horseback or by buggy along dusty roads in summer and over snowbound and storm-beaten trails in winter. As his reputation grew, he was called longer distances. Almost all of southern Minnesota became his field of practice. When operations were necessary, he performed them on the kitchen table in the patient's home, sometimes by the light of kerosene lamps held by one of the family.

Returning home one night from a difficult round of calls, Dr. Mayo sat down to a belated supper, more thoughtful than informative. His silence was unusual, and Louise took quick note of it.

"Did something go wrong today, Will?" she asked.

"Huh? Oh, wrong? Well, yes, I guess it did. I lost the Matteson boy. The little fellow who had his leg crushed by a tree. Poor child. I just couldn't stop the infection."

"The operation was extremely difficult, wasn't it?"

"Yes, hard enough. But there should be a way to overcome the morbific matter. Until we do that, medicine has still a long way to go."

"I read today in one of your scientific journals more about Lister's and Pasteur's work. They really seem to be on the track of important discoveries."

"They undoubtedly are. I've been milling it around for some time. I wonder what you will think of it?"

"What is it, Will?"

Dr. Mayo laid down his fork and leaned back in his chair, a very tired man. Louise left the kitchen stove to sit opposite him.

"Dear, I'd like to go to New York to spend a year at Bellevue Hospital. In that time I could learn enough at the medical college to do some of the things around here I know I should, but can't now. I want to see—actually see—what is being done to combat germs, what there is to this antiseptic business. The Lord knows we can use it out here."

Louise said nothing as she thought over her husband's remarks.

"Oh, I know what you're thinking, my dear," Dr. Mayo continued. "Of course, we've got to consider the children. Will's ten and Charlie's only six. The girls need a lot of things, but I think we've saved enough to keep the family going while I study in New York. You're worried though, I can see."

"No, Will, I'm not worried in the slightest. I've been wondering why I've never suggested this postgraduate work to you. It's the logical thing to do. Of course, you must go. It's the best thing in the world for all of us. Don't delay a day longer than you have to."

And so in 1871, when Dr. Mayo was nearly fifty-two years old, he interrupted his practice to learn all he could at the nation's leading medical college. There he had contact with advances in medicine and surgery he could not obtain in his remote Minnesota community. He returned enthusiastic and inspired for greater service to the people he was growing to love.

While at Bellevue, Dr. Mayo became absorbed in the microscope and the revelations it brought to science. He longed secretly to possess one, but he knew it represented an investment far beyond the family's financial capacity. He talked about it so much, however, that Louise sensed his yearning.

"Will, when are you going to buy a microscope for your work?"

"A microscope? Why, who said anything about buying a microscope? Why, Louise, don't you realize— Wouldn't it be wonderful?"

"Dad, I wish we had a microscope," young Will piped from a corner. "I've never even looked into one."

"I want a 'scope, too," Charlie chimed in. "I want a 'scope."

"Well, well, my young medical experts, you astonish me. You seem to think we're discussing a twenty-five-cent toy." Dr. Mayo tried to appear gruff. Even though he knew his sons had no understanding of what they asked, it pleased him immensely to see their interest in any apparatus pertaining to medicine.

"How much would a microscope cost, Will?" Louise asked.

"Oh, my dear, it's far too much for us to consider. One that's dependable and efficient will come to at least six hundred dollars."

"I'll give six hunnert dollars."

"Hush, Charles. Little boys are to be seen and not heard. That is a large sum, Will, but it's also a good investment. We haven't that much cash, but we do have a homestead that is good security. We can mortgage the house and raise the necessary money that way."

"Louise, you darling! Really, would you permit me to mortgage our home to get a microscope?"

"Why not? It's as important to us to have the best medical equipment as it is to have a home. Go ahead, Will, and make whatever arrangements are necessary to obtain that microscope."

In a few days Dr. Mayo had raised the required six hundred dollars and soon after became one of the country's first physicians to carry on his practice with the aid of a microscope. But it was an investment that required ten years of hard work to pay off.

Long before the debt was settled, William and Charles Mayo became familiar with the microscope and its uses. When they were still too small to handle it alone, their father lifted them into position to squint down the long drawtube through the lenses. They became experts at the instrument before some of their playmates had mastered the multiplication tables. Today the first Mayo microscope is exhibit number one in the Mayo Museum at Rochester.

While medicine was Dr. Mayo's livelihood and passion, he made politics an exciting avocation. He could no more keep his hand and voice free of civic affairs than he could stay away from a rousing political fight. His opportunities to get into lively scraps were multiplied by his minority leanings. He was a liberal Democrat in a Republican city and state.

One of his first public offices was that of coroner of Olmsted County, to which he was elected in 1869. The next year the state was stirred by a battle against the railroads, accused by one faction of monopolistic ambitions.

The fight was a natural one for Dr. Mayo to enter. He spoke at an antimonopoly meeting called in Rochester to advocate "relief from oppression imposed on the people by the railroads of Minnesota."

Chief firebrand was Ignatus Donnelly, the "sage of Mininger." Author, farmer, orator, and congressman, Donnelly, widely known as the "Apostle of Protest," attacked the Winona and St. Peter Railway for "charging exorbitant rates, discrimination in favor of wheat speculators, and general management of the road in the interest of nonresident monopolists."

Dr. Mayo and Donnelly thought alike on this subject, and when the good doctor later won election to the state senate, he was allied with the Northwest's greatest genius in the battle against the railroads.

As mayor of Rochester several times, as alderman, and then as senator for two terms, Dr. Mayo never relented in his fight on the carriers. He was ready to give or take, as the situation dictated.

Thus William and Charles Mayo spent their early childhood in an atmosphere of political strife and advancing medicine. One boy or the other, and frequently both, accompanied the doctor on long country rides to call on ailing farmers and their families. At first their duty was "to mind the horses," but when they reached the mischievous age their presence simplified their father's task of "keeping an eye on them."

Post-mortems were a special treat to which the boys were always invited. As coroner, Dr. Mayo performed many autopsies and it gave him and his sons an inexpensive means of studying anatomy. These excursions in afterdeath surgery began when the lads were so small they had difficulty in observing what was being done on the operating table.

"Get a chair or a box and stand on it," Dr. Mayo would suggest. "Hang onto something, so you won't fall off."

Having gained a point of vantage, Will and Charlie would take firm holds of the corpse, lean well forward and watch the doctor cut and probe.

When Will was sixteen, one of his father's patients had died from a complicated ailment and the doctor decided on a post-mortem to solve the puzzle. The two left home late in the evening of a stormy night to perform an autopsy. Driving across the Zumbro River to the outskirts of Rochester, they came to the Bradley House, an abandoned hotel, a remnant of frontier days. Their patient had lived alone in the building as a caretaker.

Carrying a lantern, Will pushed open the creaking door and entered the gloomy lobby. The windows of the crumbling building rattled. Dust stood thick in the corners. In a small room off the clerk's desk lay the body of the caretaker on a sagging iron bed. On a table beside the bed stood a kerosene lamp, its oil burned low. The doctor quickly lighted it. It flickered in the drafty room.

Without delay, Dr. Mayo pulled off his coat, rolled up his sleeves, and opened his instrument case. Will, too short to see well, looked about for something on which to stand.

"Go out and hunt for a box," his father said. "You might as well get a good look."

Paying no more attention to the boy, he started his examination. Two or three times the lamp was almost blown out. Occasionally the doctor spoke softly, explaining what he was doing. After an hour, he pulled out his watch and held it to the uncertain light.

"Already eleven o'clock," he grunted. "I didn't think it was so late. I've got to call on Old Man Finsted before I go home. His wife says he's in misery tonight."

Will glanced at the dissected body and offered hastily, "I'll go with you, Father."

"No, Will, you stay here and clean up everything. Sew up the incisions and then tuck that sheet around the corpse. When you finish, go right home. Take the specimens."

Wiping his hands with a soft cloth, Dr. Mayo removed the stains and then drew on his coat. He packed his instruments, picked up the bag, and walked away without another word to his son.

The door banged shut and Will Mayo stood alone beside

the pale cadaver. He shivered despite his efforts to control himself. A gust of wind struck the hotel and the ceiling timbers creaked. The windows rattled louder. The rusty hotel sign outside the door groaned ominously as it struggled in the gale.

For a moment panic gripped the future doctor. He had to fight to keep his feet from charging across the lobby. He glanced at the body again, just as the lamp flickered and almost went out. He wanted to run, run as fast as he could.

But something held him to the spot. His father had in- structed him to clean up things. He pulled a surgical needle from his coat lapel and fished into his pocket for thread. In a minute he was making rapid if unskilled stitches to close the incisions. He finished the job quickly and spent a few moments cleaning the grimy room. When it was over he felt better. With a bit of swagger, he walked out the door and headed for home.

"I'm about as proud of the fact that I *walked* out, instead of ran, as of anything else I ever made myself do," Dr. Will said many years later in telling of the experience.

A little Indian pony which Dr. Mayo presented to Will on his eighth birthday became a familiar character on Rochester's streets. Will was immensely fond and proud of his smart pet, Tony. He taught him to play hide-and-seek. The horse responded to pets and pressures that only Will could communicate. "That Mayo Boy" tore bareback up and down the streets with the speed and recklessness of the wildest Indian. He confided to playmates that he was going to be a stagecoach driver when he grew up.

Not long after he acquired his pet, Will "made the paper" when an accident befell him. The *Rochester Post* carried an item telling how "Willie" Mayo's pony had bolted, throwing off his rider. In the fall, Will broke his arm. He caught the horse, remounted, and rode home without assistance to obtain his father's ministrations. That the mishap was not due to Will's lack of horsemanship was proved when the boy a year later won second place in the county fair contest for boy riders.

Another feat that old-timers cite as typical of Will's equestrian skill took place when a circus came to Rochester. Will rode his pony downtown to see the parade. He sat proudly on his steed, high above the heads of other onlookers. Tony appeared indifferent to the colored wagons and growling wild animals. But when the elephants approached, he became excited. With a flick of his bushy tail, he jumped cleanly over a hitching rail set a few paces from the sidewalk. Just as unexpectedly, he leaped back. As though putting on a circus act, Will sat calmly on his horse, not batting an eye although the crowd scattered in fright. Will continued to watch the parade as though nothing had happened.

The pony became so responsive to Will that other riders had difficulty in managing him. This was true even of members of the Mayo family. When Will's sister, Gertrude, was nineteen she was teaching school several miles out of Rochester. Her boarding place offered far fewer comforts than her own home provided and she told her mother she would not return to her school.

"Why, Gertrude, I don't want you to do that," her mother said.

"But I won't live at that place another year."

"Perhaps you could come home nights."

"But how? It's eight miles from Rochester."

"Why couldn't you ride Will's pony? You could leave in the morning and return after school."

Will gave ready consent to the arrangement. "Sure, you can have Tony," he told Gertrude. "You'll be back after school and I can ride him then."

The first day Gertrude tried going to school with Tony was almost the last. No sooner had she got out of sight of the Mayo home than Tony rebelled. Poor Gertrude had to lead the horse most of the way out and back.

"Here, take your old pony," she said to Will that evening. "He's the stubbornest, meanest animal alive, I do believe."

"Aw now, Gertrude. Tony's all right. You just don't know how to handle him. Here—I'll show you."

Will swung to the pony's back to demonstrate. "Want to see him turn right?" Will slapped Tony gently on the nose and the horse responded at once. A light squeeze on the ribs and Tony broke into a trot. And so on through Will's repertoire of horse tricks. "He'll do anything for you when he gets used to you."

Gertrude then mounted and followed Will's instructions. Tony behaved like a gentleman. Thereafter Gertrude and Tony got on splendidly.

Will delighted in outdoor activity and physical pursuits, but Charles was of a different temperament. Even when a small boy, he was studious and could usually be found reading or writing or contriving something new. In early life he displayed a genius for making things and repairing them. When fourteen years old, he built a telescope and mounted it. Although its efficiency was somewhat in doubt, the Mayo family was very proud of Charles and his optical creation.

He obtained most of his exercise chopping wood, undoubtedly a requirement of a father who never believed in permitting hands to be idle. He split logs that farmers brought to town for the Mayo stoves and fireplace. Will attended to the sawing. Other chores around the house were divided by the brothers.

Rochester's old Central Public School provided the grade education of the brothers. The two-story brick structure in the center of one of the city's parks is now the Mayo Museum, across the street from the Clinic building. It was purchased by the Mayos to house medical exhibits which figured in the development of the Clinic to its present proportions.

While in grade school, William and Charles were not brilliant pupils. They received grades on an average with their classmates, and whenever it became a case of interest divided between geography and the circus, the circus always won.

Charles's passion to watch "the greatest show on earth" come to town led to an escapade typical of the boy. When he and Charles Ellison, who later became a Rochester judge, were about ten years old, they decided to be the first to see the show wagons enter the city.

In those days circuses traveled by wagon from one show place to another. The night before one was due, Charles and young Ellison plotted to start out next morning to meet the train.

Without a word to their parents, they set out afoot at 4 A.M. They walked miles into the country before encountering the gaudy red carts rumbling down the dusty road. They forgot their weariness in their excitement.

When the train caught up to them, the driver of the big wild animal wagon stopped. "Hey, ya kids, what are ya doing way out here?" he called.

"We—we wanted to see the circus, first," Charles replied.

"Well, you've seen it. Now come on up here and ride her into town."

Breathless, the boys clambered aboard and sat beside the driver, popeyed with joy. Back into Rochester they bounced and swayed, the envy of every lad in town.

While the formal education of the Mayo boys was like that of their playmates, they were absorbing from their father a unique but practical knowledge of medicine. Seldom did Dr. Mayo start on his round of calls without a young "teamster" beside him. The boys were taken into the sickrooms, where they watched their father test and probe, examine and treat. On the way to the next call, the doctor explained what he had done and why and what was likely to happen.

As their medical knowledge increased, the boys were permitted to have a part in the doctor's work. They were taught how to twist and wax linen thread for ligatures. Frequently they stepped in during operations to mop blood from a wound. And they had to do this without getting in the way of the "old doc."

The Mayos' reputation to a degree was founded on their success with new and daring types of surgery. As a country physician, Dr. Mayo had to handle whatever emergency arose as best he could. Ingenuity often outweighed precedent. He had just returned from his year's study at Bellevue Hospital with an *ad eundem* degree when he had a chance to test his new knowledge. His feat is a part of the Mayo annals.

An Anesthetist at Twelve

R. MAYO USUALLY WAS CALLED to treat the most desperate cases—cases that puzzled the oldest medical heads of the region. He gave up none as hopeless, however, until he had exhausted every trick and wile of his versatile skill. He was the "pioneer surgeon of the Northwest" in a double sense.

One morning he was visited by Jacob Waggoner, a dark-skinned blacksmith whose grim expression told of a deep-seated worry. As he entered Dr. Mayo's office, he reeked with the scent of horses and sweat and the musty fumes of the forge.

"Hello, Jake," the doctor said. "What's the trouble? Lost your best friend?"

"Doc, it's my wife. She's got a big swelling, down here,

and she's in pain all the time. It's killing her. We had a couple of other doctors to see her, but they didn't help any. You've got to do something for her. Come over today, will you?"

"Certainly, Jake. I'll be out this afternoon."

"Thanks, Doc. If you can't do something for her, I guess nobody can. The others say it's hopeless."

Dr. Mayo found the blacksmith's wife suffering from an ovarian tumor. It was the kind of medical problem given up as beyond aid by most practitioners. Only specialists in the Eastern medical centers attempted to correct the ailment.

"Well, Jake, I want to tell you it's bad," Dr. Mayo said after he had completed his examination and retired from the sickroom. "There's only one chance to save her. But it is a chance."

"What's that, Doc? She can't stand this much longer. She'd rather be dead than to suffer like she does."

"All right, Jake. Then we'll operate."

"Operate?"

"Yes, that's the only thing that will save her now."

"But it's dangerous, isn't it?"

"Of course. But there's nothing else to do, I tell you."

"Have you operated on a case like this before?"

"No, I haven't, Jake, but I'm ready to do the best I can. I tell you, it's the only thing left to do. Go in, talk it over with the missus."

Jacob Waggoner was gone a long time. When he again confronted Dr. Mayo the gloom had not vanished from his face.

"Well, all right, Doc. She said no at first, but she can't live in misery like she is. If you can save her by operating, praise the Lord."

"Very well, Jake. You'll have to help me by making some things. Now, here's what I want," the doctor said as he accompanied the smith to his shop, giving detailed instructions for fashioning several instruments needed in the operation. In a few hours, the blacksmith had made from teeth of a mowing machine a set of clamps fitted with hooks.

In this instance, as in others, the little doctor faced something new, and he had to rely on his experience and practical understanding to obtain equipment for his pioneer surgery. When everything was ready, Dr. Mayo returned to the blacksmith's home with three other doctors and Louise, his wife. She often assisted him in his work, and Mrs. Waggoner's case was one requiring every possible aid.

In the kitchen of the Waggoner home, with Will and Charlie peering through the door, Dr. Mayo performed the first abdominal operation for ovarian tumor ever attempted in Minnesota. To his own delight, as well as the Waggoners' thanksgiving, his first use of the clamp method was a success. The feat established Dr. Mayo's good reputation. He performed thirty-one laparotomies of this type before retiring from practice.

Will's and Charlie's initiation as actual surgical assistants, when they were boys of sixteen and twelve years, was not exactly unforeseen, but it came when it did largely by chance. For some time, Will was the "scrub nurse" for his father's operations. Charlie, who was short for his twelve years, was already efficient in sterilizing the operating instruments. He kept them ready in the charcoal furnace of a soldering outfit. Moreover, he served, with considerable professional pride, as a mobile surgical cabinet by keeping suture thread and strands of catgut dangling from his coat buttons and lapels within easy reach of the doctor. He would display on the slightest encouragement his skill in threading surgical needles.

Both boys were free from school one late spring day when Dr. Mayo suggested they accompany him into the country to help in an operation. The task was unusually difficult and the doctor engaged another Rochester physician to assist him. When the four reached the farm home several miles outside the city, Charlie immediately set up his sterilizing outfit and Will prepared for his "scrub nurse" duties. The woman patient was carried to the kitchen table and the assisting doctor began to administer the anesthetic.

Soon after Dr. Mayo had made an incision, his medical helper was overcome by ether fumes and fainted. The situation was critical. Dr. Mayo could not drop his scalpel. The patient strained and struggled in pain. Will was busy mopping the wound. The doctor glanced at Charlie tending to his sterilizing furnace.

"Charlie! Give her more ether, quick!" Dr. Mayo called.

The boy ran to the head of the table. He picked up the ether cone, but was too short to hold it over the woman's face.

"Get the crackerbox over there," his father said. "What's the matter with you? Can't you hurry?"

The lad, whose playmates were at that moment shooting marbles or fishing in the Zumbro River, met the emergency. He set the box beside the patient and climbed upon it.

"When I raise my finger, give her ether," the doctor ordered. "When I shake my head, stop."

Watching for his father's signals, Charlie dipped ether slowly until a shake of the head checked him. When the doctor was too preoccupied with the operation to give instructions, Charlie eyed the patient for his cue. As soon as the farmer's wife stopped struggling he shut off the anesthetic. He let it drip again when she showed signs of consciousness. Once the boy became so interested in the operation he set down the ether cone. He leaned far over to see what was being done.

"Charlie!"

The sharp rebuke startled the boy so that he nearly toppled from his box. Thereafter he paid stricter attention to his task, although he was far more interested in his father's.

From this and subsequent experiences, the Mayo boys knew more when they entered medical school than most seniors. The Mayo family never had a doubt about the future career of the boys. It was taken for granted by all that they would follow in their father's path.

"There was never any question of our lifework," Will once said. "We never thought of doing anything else."

Even when the boys were still too young to consider medical school, the parents laid plans for their future education. Mrs. Mayo insisted, and the doctor agreed wholeheartedly, that no expense or effort should be spared toward that end.

From her Scotch parentage, Mrs. Mayo inherited strong character, broad charity, and good sense. Her intellectual interests were the awe of the good women of Rochester of that early time. They could never understand her, "wasting her time on astronomy," which she studied with a telescope largely of her own construction. Botany was another subject about which she knew more than most teachers. What time Dr. Mayo lacked for reading scientific journals was made up by his wife, who perused them systematically. She could discuss with her husband almost any problem of medicine or surgery. Mrs. Mayo served as the balance wheel for her impulsive husband. She kept within proper bounds his flagrant generosity by her clear, decisive justice and sound logic.

Dr. Mayo was largely influential in Will's and Charlie's choice of reading. He was often found sitting on a stool in the book-lined Mayo living room, one volume under his arm, another held between his knees while he thumbed a third, searching for some reference he wanted the boys to see.

"Our father encouraged us in reading Sir Walter Scott's novels for historical background and Dickens for a grounding in sociological subjects," Will recalled. "I can still remember passages from Haeckel, read as a young boy."

After they completed their grade courses in Central Public School, the boys attended Niles Academy, a private preparatory school conducted in one of Rochester's office buildings.

Despite the growing Mayo practice, the family bank account never was so great that the children were pampered. Mrs. Mayo followed the custom of the day of cutting down her husband's clothes to fit Will, who handed them down to Charlie.

Then, one glorious day, Charlie received his first suit of "store clothes," the gift of Will. The elder brother had obtained a vacation job in a Rochester drugstore, where he learned to compound prescriptions. From his earnings he purchased for Charlie a coat and pants, matched.

"I was mighty proud," Charlie said in telling of his boyhood. "I'll never forget that suit. Wish I had it yet."

Recognizing the need for bringing the physicians of the state together for mutual enlightenment and protection, Dr. Mayo was one of the founders of the Minnesota State Medical Society in 1870. Within three years he was elected president.

He took advantage of every opportunity to enhance his practice and broaden his field of operations. His stable was confined to two or three horses of questionable breed in those first years at Rochester. So he gladly accepted the offer to ride with a parish priest, who made his calls behind a magnificent span of fast trotters. That priest was later Msgr. William Riordan, a well-known Minnesota clergyman. He and Dr. Mayo were familiar figures riding together over their medical and spiritual circuits.

The advances in medicine which Dr. Mayo and other physicians were bringing to the community were not accepted without some question by the oldsters, who infrequently sought medical advice. One such skeptic, Brick Jack Campion, stopped Dr. Mayo and Father Riordan on the street one day to question them.

"What's medicine coming to, with all these changes going on?" Campion asked.

"What do you mean?" Dr. Mayo asked.

"Well, Doc, it was a lot different when I was a boy. Whenever a Campion got sick, we sent for only three things —Old Doc Mayo, Father Riordan, and a jug of whisky."

Dr. Mayo delighted in feuds, and while his ammunition was not as deadly as deer-rifle bullets, he would parry penpoint for penpoint, day or night.

His chief opponent was a farm-implement dealer, John Edgar, who also loaned money and battled for the Republican and prohibition causes. Dr. Mayo could never be suspected of being a prohibitionist. He loved sociability and congenial company too much. Consequently, Mr. Edgar and Dr. Mayo exchanged spicy letters in the Rochester weekly. When the issues were too far apart to suit their tempers, they printed broadsides and distributed them around the community.

Dr. Mayo's candidacy for the mayoralty in 1882 was marked by especially brilliant verbal pyrotechnics. Despite the fervent opposition of Edgar and his friends, Dr. Mayo won the election. At his inaugural, the good doctor found the occasion fit and proper to express his candid opinion of his foes. In his speech he said:

"I am proud to be called a bummer and a disorganizer, when it comes from a vulgar, wealthy man of flyblown reputation, who has obtained riches by questionable means and who, like Ananias of old, took the purchase money. But that notorious ancestor in a true Christian spirit of restitution went out and hanged himself."

The next week's issue of the paper contained Edgar's answer. He called attention first to Dr. Mayo's new version of the Scripture and suggested he probably was referring to Judas. Mr. Edgar then opined that the doctor was better acquainted with the tactics of Ananias than anyone in Rochester. He proposed that Dr. Mayo be made the sole dictator of the community, giving him "all the business of pills and powders and let him have a monopoly on all the curing and killing. Make him the sole ruler of the city and the only doctor in the county."

The printed invective got out of hand and "Veritas" in the next week's edition voiced the public desire for "a rest from another deluge of slang and abuse from Mayo and Edgar."

As mayor, Dr. Mayo used his office to war on cure-alls and quacks who found Rochester a fertile field for their nostrums. The fakery inflicted upon the suffering infuriated him to the boiling point. His modest business cards on the inside pages of Rochester's newspapers were lost in the glare of lurid front-page advertisements of patent medicines which would "positively cure neuralgia, influenza, sore and bleeding lungs, hoarseness, cough, rheumatism, diarrhea, dysentery, cholera morbus, kidney troubles, diseases of the spine and lame back."

The time was nearing for Will to begin his medical education at college. Both he and Charlie were earning modest sums working during vacation months in Geisinger and Newton's drugstore. With his savings and his father's help, Will could finance his advanced schooling. He was nineteen, in 1880, when he and the doctor decided the University of Michigan offered the medical subjects he wanted. The course recently had been changed from two to three years and was rated high in the profession.

Will was at Ann Arbor only a short time before the professors were attracted to him. Here was an unusual student. He could handle a microscope and he had a knowledge of anatomy. Before long, Will Mayo was a student assistant in dissection to Professor Corydon L. Ford. He received his surgical training under Professor Donald Maclean, famous teacher who had studied under Syms in Edinburgh and had associated with Joseph Lister, father of modern surgery.

Finished with his medical course in three years, Dr. Will returned to Rochester and at the age of twenty-two became associated with his father in general medical practice. There was no requirement in the 1880's that a physician must serve a period as a hospital intern. In fact, hospitals were few and those few considered a necessary evil.

It was an era of professional smugness. Doctors dressed to impress the observer with their importance. A frock coat and top hat were considered correct street wear. Youthful physicians grew beards and mustaches to give age and experience to their appearance. But Dr. Will scorned such accouterment. He shaved, wore a felt hat, and his business suit was no different from that of the city's druggists and merchants.

The style adopted by the new doctor was not a confession of an inferiority complex, however. At a party which Dr. Will attended shortly after his return home in June 1883 with his M.D. degree, he was approached by Judge Charles M. Start, who later became a state supreme-court justice.

"Congratulations, Dr. Mayo," he said. "Now that you're a full-fledged doctor, I suppose you'll look around for an opening in a large city—Chicago or New York, perhaps."

"No, judge, I expect to remain in Rochester and become the greatest surgeon in the world."

Dr. Will was accepted in Rochester as a valued member of the community. The Mayo business card in the *Rochester Record and Union* made official the association of father and son in the medical practice.

Charles was only eighteen and would not go to college for another two years. Nevertheless, he was already an active partner in the Mayo business and before long was to have, with his brother and father, an important role in a major event that was destined to spread the fame of the trio.

CHAPTER EIGHT

Mercy Rides a Tornado

HERE WAS AN OPPRESSIVE
listlessness about the day. It was late August and it was hot,
excessively so. About four o'clock in the afternoon a light
shower fell, but it only added to the feeling that before the
day was out something evil would strike Rochester. The
wind that eddied in fitful gusts failed to quicken the spirit.

A prophetic stillness fell over the community at seven
o'clock. The citizens of Rochester left their supper tables
mopping their brows and watching with concern the tum-
bling black clouds crowding over the southwestern horizon.
Occasional spurts of lightning, with delayed rumbles of
thunder, etched a menacing backdrop for the approaching
storm.

The clouds crowded each other in three levels. The top tier was tinged a ghastly green. The center was almost black. Whisps of gray scudded before the bottom layer hugging the earth.

Two young men driving northward from the city in a shiny phaeton tried to hide from each other their thoughts about the nearing storm. Their swift backward glances at the greasy clouds revealed their anxiety.

"Charlie, I don't like the looks of it," Dr. Will Mayo said to his brother.

"Does look kind of threatening."

"I think we'd better turn back. We can come out to the slaughterhouse tomorrow to get the sheep's eyes. My experiments with cataract operations can wait."

"Sure, the sheep's eyes can wait," Charlie said. "Here's a place to turn around. Come on, Midge, let's get home. We don't want to get a soaking."

The Mayo brothers swung around quickly and urged their swift mare into a trot. From the top of the slope that marked the northern boundaries of the city of five thousand Yankee, Irish, German, and Norwegian settlers, they could see several grain elevators on a siding of the Winona and St. Peter Railway. The railroad station and two-stall engine house and repair shop were just visible to the east.

In front of them crawled the Zumbro River, which provided power for the city's flour mill. The Harvester works employing seventy-five men squatted a little distance downstream. The brothers were familiar with the frame and brick stores with their false fronts that lay beyond the barrier of trees before them. Daily they trod the business district's planked sidewalks and drove their horses through its dirt streets.

Now, of a sudden, a great peril had come to all this, their home town, to their family. They raced back to seek refuge among its friendly dwellings and tree-lined streets. They were driven by an uncontrollable fright. As they urged their mare to greater speed, the brothers heard a noise like a distant freight train lumbering across a trestle. With a leap, the black cloud was over them. A vicious, writhing tail dropped to the earth and dusted the farmlands a mile to the west.

"She's a tornado, Will!" Charlie called in a tight voice. "Look at that black funnel!"

"It's heading right for us!" Will cried. "Get going, Midge! Hurry! Giddap! Giddap!"

Pounding across the Zumbro River bridge, the galloping Midge jerked the Mayo brothers into Rochester just as the twister hit the outskirts of the city. The funnel, small at the bottom and large at the top, shrieked across the northern half of the community. A yellowish mist swirled high into the air. With a jarring crunch, the bridge collapsed and dropped into the river. The Mayos were the last ones to cross. As they sped over the railroad tracks, they looked west in time to see a large grain elevator topple onto the rails. By now the din was ear-splitting. Boards, shingles, debris of all kinds flew everywhere. Freight cars rumbled down the tracks before the wind and then leaped crazily, some falling into the millrace.

Dashing into the city, the brothers whirled around the corner of the Cook House just as a cornice, sixteen feet long, dropped upon them. It struck the horse, broke the shafts and nearly knocked the animal to the ground. The brothers escaped death by inches. Turning into an alley, they urged the injured mare on. Just before they reached a small blacksmith shop, the tin roof blew off and rolled down the alley toward them.

Trembling, Midge hugged the wall. The brothers did likewise. A confusion of sound and destruction held them prisoner and they cowered helpless in the wind, amid the blinding lightning and the drenching rain.

In a few minutes the greedy gale roared away to lash at grain stacks, farm buildings, and rural dwellings. Behind, it left Rochester's "Lower Town" a ruin. The towering elevators were knocked flat, sprawled over the railroad tracks. The railroad station stood without roof. The Harvester works was a wreck; the flour mill was ripped apart. Tin roofs pulled from shops and stores clattered and banged and then lay still in the streets like furrows of scorched hay.

Between two and three hundred homes were torn and battered in that cyclonic blast. Property loss amounted to half a million dollars. But that was the minor part of the tragedy that struck Rochester that August 21, 1883.

The city faced an emergency it could barely meet. The storm had taken the lives of twenty-two persons. Their course had been run. But the several hundred who had been injured, among them sixty seriously, presented a problem new to Rochester. It had never been called upon to cope with such mass suffering.

It had no hospital in which to care for the injured. Dr. William W. Mayo, nearing his sixty-fifth birthday, Dr. Will Mayo, then twenty-two, a few other physicians and surgeons comprised the only medical force in the city able to treat the wounded. There wasn't a trained nurse in the whole community. Primitive, emergency measures had to be taken.

As soon as the tornado passed, Dr. Will and Charlie hurried to their home over debris-littered streets. When a block away, they saw their dwelling had been spared. Their father had already reached home.

"Thank God, you boys are safe," he exclaimed. "I knew you had gone to the slaughterhouse and I was afraid you'd been caught. We must be thankful all of us are well. But we've got to help the others. Will, Charlie, this is an evil night for Rochester. Come with me."

The old doctor and his sons hurried to the business district. They found a group of excited citizens discussing their plight. Others came from the storm area bearing injured and dying victims. Several were carried into Dr. Mayo's office, others into private homes. Soon the stream of sufferers became overwhelming.

"Something must be done to care for these poor people," Dr. Mayo said to the panic-stricken citizens. "Open Rommel's hall. Get every cot and bed you can spare. Bring all the bedding you can lay your hands on. We've got to fix up some kind of hospital. Get as many women as you can to help as nurses."

As quickly as they were set up, the beds and cots were filled with the injured. Tossing aside their coats, Dr. Mayo, Will, and Charlie gave their attention to the most desperate cases. In an improvised operating room, they amputated arms and legs, set broken bones, sewed up wounds. It was a desperate task, calling for speedy surgery, hasty treatment.

When the medical work was at its height, Dr. Mayo was interrupted by one of the women helping to care for the injured. "Doctor, Mother Mary Alfred Moes is here to speak to you a moment. Will you come?"

Glancing up from his task, Dr. Mayo brushed his hand across his tired face. In the wavering kerosene lamplight he saw a woman in black approach. He recognized her as one of the twenty-five Franciscan nuns who, as the Sisters of St. Francis, five years before had established in Rochester the academy for girls and convent of Our Lady of Lourdes.

"Dr. Mayo, we sisters of the academy would like to help you. There are four of us here, ready to serve as nurses, if you can use us."

"Oh thank you, Sister. We surely do need your help. Thank you, thank you! There is so much to be done. Please come this way."

Through the long, agonizing night, the three Mayos and the other Rochester doctors labored. The four sisters were invaluable assistants. The most desperate cases were kept at Rommel's hall, the others placed in private homes. Shelter was found for those whose dwellings had been wrecked. The city council in emergency session placed Dr. Mayo in charge of all physicians caring for the injured.

A reporter in the *Rochester Post* described the storm scene in this manner: "The work of the storm fiend is complete. He gave no quarter to man, woman or dimpled child. No home, no family escaped his wrath. The death angel was enthroned above his dusky form and together with a wild, hideous roar, they swept down upon our beautiful city like a devouring demon.

"An hour later the pale moonbeams fell upon a hundred ruined homes, a score of dead upturned faces, and the night air was filled with the shrieks and groaning of the wounded and dying."

In the week that followed, the doctors gave every waking hour to caring for the tornado victims. Most of them began a slow convalescence in the cramped quarters of the meeting hall. The equipment was scant and every convenience of a hospital was missing.

As Dr. Mayo was making a morning visit to the hall, he was approached by Mother Superior Mary Alfred. Her pale face bore a serious expression and she gazed at the old doctor for several moments before daring to speak. Summoning her courage, she broached the subject closest to her heart.

"Dr. Mayo, I wonder whether the people of Rochester really appreciate the great work you and the other physicians have done here."

The old doctor looked at her in surprise. "Why, there's nothing so great about it. We took care of the injured as best we could."

"Yes, as best you could. You did a fine thing with the few facilities you had. That leads me to what I want to suggest. Doctor, don't you think it would be a fine thing, a wonderful thing, if Rochester had a hospital?"

"A hospital? Yes, perhaps. But Mother Superior, hospitals are costly to build. They are expensive to operate. They require considerable capital. I'm afraid Rochester is too small to support one."

"But the tornado demonstrated the great need."

"Yes, there is a need, obviously, but where is the money coming from to build it?"

"Ways could be found."

"I assure you, it would be too difficult a job to build one here. And even if we had one, there would be no assurance of its success."

"Dr. Mayo, I believe you are wrong about that. And I think I can prove it to you. All I ask is that you make one promise."

"What is it?"

"If you will promise to take charge, the sisters of St. Francis will build a hospital."

"Oh, but Mother Superior, you forget. I'm an old man— I'm nearly sixty-five. I probably haven't many years left to practice."

"True, Doctor, but you have two sons. One already is a physician and the other will be before long. They can carry on when you leave off."

Dr. Mayo stood thoughtful for a long time. He looked sharply at the Mother Superior and saw the determination stamped on her face.

"Mother Mary Alfred, your faith and your hope must not be disappointed. Give me a little time to investigate this matter. Perhaps something can be made of your idea."

"Thank you, Dr. Mayo. Please draw your plans. We will see that the hospital is built."

Before many weeks passed, Dr. Mayo was convinced the city should have a hospital. He obtained the deed to a fourteen-acre apple orchard owned by John D. Ostrum beyond the western limits of the city and turned it over to the Franciscan sisters.

The start of the great St. Mary's Hospital, which was to become the historic scene of the Mayo surgical triumphs, had been made.

The task the religious order faced taxed it for years. While the sisters skimped and saved to raise the seventy-five thousand dollars set as the contract price for the first St. Mary's Hospital, the old doctor drew and redrew plans for the structure. He and Dr. Will traveled to Chicago and to the East to study hospital construction and to incorporate the best features in the sisters' venture.

While the nuns spent the next years acquiring a few dollars here, a few hundred there, Will and Charlie Mayo were sinking the roots that were to nourish their surgical careers. Occasional items that appeared in the *Rochester Record and Union* of that period hint at the growing prominence of Dr. Will.

The following notice ran September 7, shortly after the tornado struck: "Dr. Will Mayo cut a cataract from the eye of Mrs. Tean Wednesday. It was the second operation of this kind ever performed in the city."

A little more than a year later, on November 20, 1884, Will married Hattie M. Damon, daughter of Eleazer Damon, pioneer watchmaker and jeweler of Rochester. It was hardly a society event, since the news was given a mere notice in the paper's personal column. Dr. Will spent the next two months in New York with his bride, taking advanced medical training at the Polyclinic Postgraduate Medical School.

Charlie, three years out of high school, was finally ready, in his father's eyes, to begin his formal medical education in 1885.

The *Record and Union* on September 23 carried this note: "Dr. W. W. Mayo and his son Charles went to Chicago two days ago when Charles entered Chicago Medical College." A week later the paper had this item: "Dr. W. W. Mayo returned from Chicago yesterday after seeing his son Charles enter Chicago Medical College, where he will study for three years. Dr. William James Mayo and wife left today for New York where Dr. Mayo will attend classes at Polyclinic, a postgraduate school. They will be gone several months."

Dr. Will's constant quest for medical knowledge is a saga of travel in search for information. He scoured the world for new methods and techniques of surgery. He crossed the

Atlantic thirty-four times to witness the work of great European surgeons. Once he made a trip to Australia to observe a new technique of an incision. Even when busy with their practice in Rochester, the brothers always took time for study. For some years they spent alternate week ends in Chicago to attend the famous teaching clinic conducted by Dr. Christian Fenger, father of modern surgery in the west.

Charles's return to Rochester as a doctor of medicine was duly recorded in the newspaper. He completed his training in March 1888. The *Record and Union* carried the following note: "Charlie Mayo has graduated from a long course of study in medicine and surgery, which with his experience in a drugstore of two years and more, gives him nearly six years of hard work in preparation. He will enter practice with his father and brother, making the firm W. W., W. J. and C. H. Mayo."

The next year, Dr. Charlie went to New York to attend the Polyclinic Postgraduate School and won another M.D. degree. He was given a special certificate in 1890 for work done at the New York Postgraduate Medical School.

Thus the Mayo triumvirate was a going concern, ready to staff the projected hospital as soon as the twenty-five Franciscan nuns could finance it. The sisters managed, by the summer of 1888, to present their contractor with the needed seventy-five thousand dollars and work was started.

Up to this time, Dr. Mayo performed some of his operations in a small private hospital opened after the tornado by a Mrs. Carpenter, a practical nurse. More often his surgery took place in homes or in a small special hotel for hospital guests. It had no operating room and the work had to be done in the patient's quarters.

The opening of the sisters' three-story hospital, christened St. Mary's, on September 30, 1889, made available forty beds in three wards and one private room. From the experience he had gained in his practice and from his travels, Dr. Mayo designed the hospital's first operating room.

Thirteen patients were registered on the first day. The doctors Mayo, W. W., Will, and Charlie, made up the medical staff. A corps of six Franciscan sisters, Mary Joseph, Hyacinth, Constantine, Sylvester, Sienna, and Sidelis, comprised the nursing force.

Dr. Mayo was seventy years old and aware that he would soon have to pass on to his sons the burden he had carried so successfully for so many years. Doctors Will and Charlie were just starting their careers, neither with hospital-intern experience.

With some misgivings they took up the responsibility thrust upon them. They felt themselves "the greenest of a green crew," but that very circumstance made them all the more cautious and watchful. They weighed every suggestion for organization and management of the fledgling institution and exercised reverent care in the performance of their medical work.

The hospital's first patient was an operative case for an eye tumor. The young doctors made elaborate preparations for their initial test. Their seventy-year-old father was the anesthetist and the entire nursing staff was in attendance. One nurse, Sister Mary Joseph, for almost half a century was the guiding spirit of the hospital. As Mary Dempsey of Rochester she had taken the habit in 1878 and became a teacher at a Catholic mission in Ashland, Kentucky. Her unusual abilities were observed by Mother Mary Alfred, and when the mother superior took charge of the new hospital, she recalled Sister Mary Joseph to assume nursing duties. In this role she later won the praise of the Mayos as the "first of our splendid assistants."

Although Rochester at last had a hospital, it lacked the facilities looked upon today as fundamental. There was no telephone service and the doctors were summoned by messengers, who came by horse and buggy or afoot.

The only lights were kerosene lamps, which the sisters carried about at night. An oil lantern hung on a tree outside the doorway to guide the doctors when returning from late calls. There was no elevator and the patients had to be carried up and down the stairways. The operating table was the product of Charlie's inventive genius and served the hospital until an improved one could be imported from Germany two years later.

It was in such a bare setting, with much equipment of their own devising, that the Mayo brothers started their surgical practice that one day was to fill a dozen hospitals and require the services of hundreds of physicians and surgeons and more hundreds of staff workers to care for the sick and suffering who came from every part of the world.

CHAPTER NINE

Hospital Run on Unique Policy

LTHOUGH GIVING FULL
heart and skill to the new project, the elder Mayo could
not allay his misgivings over the hospital. He feared the
Catholic sisters' large investment would prove extravagant
and unprofitable.

One day, soon after the hospital opened, he voiced his
concern to Mother Mary Alfred.

"Mother Mary, I hope St. Mary's Hospital gets enough
patients to make a profit," he said. "They ought to come
from Eyota, Plainview, and Oronoco, as well as from Rochester."

"Dr. Mayo, I have no worries about that. I'm convinced
the sick in the neighboring towns will use the facilities you
have helped to build here."

"I certainly hope so. If this hospital should fail, I would feel I misguided you."

"Please don't worry about it, Dr. Mayo. We have a fine institution and I'm sure it will succeed."

Dr. Mayo lived to see St. Mary's Hospital enlarged and expanded to care for scores and then hundreds who came for the ministrations of the Mayos and their hospital assistants. Virtually from the day it opened, it filled a great need. After the first period of trial, the question of finances never pressed the faithful sisters.

At the beginning the three Mayos attended to all the medical duties in the hospital. They were its only surgeons, and after a hard day's work of operations, office consultations, and calls on the sick they returned at night to nurse male patients.

The task of climbing three flights of stairs many times daily irked Dr. Charlie. He said the hospital needed an elevator. The way to get one was to build one, he decided. Accordingly, with the help of Fred Livermore, a Rochester machinist, he dug a deep hole for the "plunger" and rigged a cage that ran from the basement to the top floor.

It had one serious disadvantage, however. It could be operated only from the inside. Since the hospital could not yet afford an elevator man, Will or Charlie or a nurse had to run up and down stairs to find where the lift rested and bring it to the desired landing. But it proved its worth in saving the patients many a weary and painful step.

Before the hospital opened, the St. Francis sisters discussed with the Mayos a policy of operation. The three doctors, Mother Mary Alfred, and Sister Mary Joseph were free in voicing their opinions.

"I believe a hospital should give care to all patients, regardless of his or her financial condition," Dr. Mayo suggested. "I believe charity and paying patients should be treated alike."

"That certainly would be an innovation in hospital management," Dr. Will said. "But it might prove a strain on the sisters, financially."

"I am glad to hear you suggest such a policy, Dr. Mayo," the Mother Superior interrupted. "That has always been my thought, ever since we started this project."

"You must remember that sickness and poverty are close allies," Dr. Charlie said. "You may have more charity than paying patients under such a system. But please understand me. I agree such a policy is commendable. In fact, it's the finest thing you could do. But you can't afford to be too lenient."

"I have found in my long experience that patients will pay for medical treatment if they have any means with which to do so," the elder Mayo added. "I don't believe you need to worry about the finances. Of course, there are many who haven't a cent and can't pay hospital and doctor bills. On the other hand, a good many poor folks will skimp to meet their sickness expenses. I truly believe that the suggested policy will be a profitable one, as well as a great humanitarian step."

"That's the way it shall be," the sisters agreed.

St. Mary's Hospital thus inaugurated its system of caring for the sick of every rank, regardless of their financial position. The patient's need and not his bank account was to determine the care and treatment he received.

The same policy, carried out to an even greater extreme,

guided the Mayo practice. Its success is evident in the gigantic St. Mary's Hospital of today and the skyscraper Mayo Clinic that symbolizes medical progress.

By the end of 1890, its first complete year, St. Mary's had treated three hundred patients and thirty were still confined there. It had not been swamped with charity patients, despite its unique policy. Even in that first year it was self-supporting.

The surgical success of the young Mayos was quick to win recognition. Death took less than two per cent of the patients on which they operated, an almost unheard-of ratio. The doctors soon had a local reputation for their ingenuity and skill in the operating room. That reputation did not long remain one of so limited a scope.

It was the good fortune of the Mayos to begin their careers at a time when surgery was entering new fields. It was armed with two new and powerful weapons—anesthetics and antiseptics. The young surgeons had attended medical colleges at the time these advanced aids were receiving emphasis and recognition. They were young enough to dare to experiment with them and to further their application. Surgery was in the ascendancy and they rode the wave.

Since their practice kept pace with the phenomenal success of the new hospital, the Mayos found it necessary to enlarge their private establishment. The father maintained a dozen fine horses in his stable. He was never certain how long, after a hard trip, before he would be called out again. He wanted fresh and rested horses ready at all times.

While the elder Mayo had good teams, Dr. Will demanded and had nothing but the fastest and finest obtainable. He refused to own one that could not travel twelve to fifteen miles an hour, and for several hours. Rochester was the center of a brisk horse-trading region and became known as the Lexington of the Northwest. Good stock was imported and Rochester's state fair attracted horse lovers from all over the United States.

When on the highway making sick calls, the old doctor demanded and invariably obtained the right of way. He raced along at top speed and when he overtook a lagging vehicle, he announced himself loudly. Every driver in Olmsted County knew the Mayo voice. When he heard its roar, he immediately pulled far to one side and let the doctor pass.

Dr. Charlie, in his early experiences at St. Mary's, never allowed a new problem, mechanical or surgical, to master him. He put the spirit of the inventor into his work. Whenever he lacked instruments for a special operation, he devised his own. Whenever a surgical puzzle made necessary some new or untried technique, he worked out his own method. One of the most unusual was that presented by a huge Norwegian woodsman who came to the hospital soon after it opened. He suffered from a goiter so large it forced his head back. It extended from under his chin to the middle of his breastbone.

Dr. Charlie blinked his soft brown eyes in astonishment and sat down to think it over. He had never before seen such an enormous goiter, much less heard of a way to remove it. Whenever possible, he applied the simplest and most obvious method of treatment. Using this theory, he literally shucked the growth from its pod.

He described what he did in this manner: "I split the thing from top to bottom and the hardy Norwegian had enough blood left to live, although we didn't think he would. I put on a tight pack and next day the goiter had started to shuck itself from its capsule. With just a little help, it popped out and the man got well right away. I was projected in that way into operation on the thyroid gland."

That was Dr. Charlie's first goiter operation without anesthesia. In his long years of practice he performed five thousand more. By 1935, more than twenty-seven thousand goiter patients had passed through Mayo Clinic. Dr. Charlie's technique is credited with reducing the death rate in this class of cases by one-half. The daring displayed by Dr. Charlie in his attack on unfamiliar surgical tasks was shared by his brother. Dr. Will never hesitated to attempt the unusual when a life was at stake. The Mayos and their feats were news and the Rochester newspapers printed frequent items about them.

One such paragraph about their work, appearing about this time, follows: "Dr. W. J. Mayo saved the life of a daughter of Christ Figerson last week by inserting a tube in her throat when she was nearly suffocated with croup. The operation was a complete success and the tube was removed the first of the week."

Soon after, another item said: "Last Sunday Dr. W. J. Mayo, assisted by Drs. C. H. Mayo, A. W. Stinchfield, Ida Clark and Homer Collins removed an ovarian tumor weighing forty pounds from Mrs. Jacob Stark of Kasson. She is reported to be recovering."

Evidence that the elder Mayo still held his high professional reputation is contained in a newspaper item, as follows: "Dr. W. W. Mayo was called to St. Paul for a consultation with other doctors on a serious case."

The publicity given the Mayos could hardly remain universally favorable, especially since the old doctor was perennially in the political field. He seemed to be running for office at every election. In 1890, after serving two terms as mayor of Rochester and as alderman, he became a candidate for the state senate. Dr. Mayo's political alliance with the Democratic party made him a shining target for the *Rochester Post*, a Republican sheet, which never missed an opportunity to sink its bitterest barbs into the Mayo hide, no matter how much it respected his medical skill.

The winning of a senate seat was a matter of personal moment to the elder Mayo. A few years before he had run for the post and lost it by a single vote. It was generally acknowledged his defeat was due to the absence of his name from the ballot in several neighboring towns.

A political convention of Democrats, leagued with the Farmers Alliance, was scheduled for Rochester in the 1890 campaign. The *Post* reported the gathering in this manner: "As soon as it was known Dr. Mayo would address the convention, there was a general stampede for the door and when he arrived at the hall, less than one-fourth of the delegates remained. If the reader has ever listened to one of the doctor's harangues, he can imagine what was said on this occasion." For good measure, the *Post* added: "He [Dr. Mayo] has the most vindictive and abusive tongue in Olmsted County. He has never made a rational speech in his life."

Despite the *Post's* plea to the electorate to "snow under the agitator and demagogue Mayo, so that he will never get out again," the candidate won. It was a veritable landslide of votes cast by the Democrats and the antimonopoly farmers. The doctor's fight on the railroads was too popular to be denied.

Dr. Charlie had been nominated for Olmsted County coroner on the same ticket, but he promptly withdrew when notified. He, as well as Dr. Will, was too busy with medicine to give time to—to say nothing of relishing—a political scrap.

While the opening of St. Mary's Hospital gave the Mayos an important ally in their medical practice, it added to their long hours, since they maintained their downtown office and answered calls all over the county. Their business card of 1890 gave the address of their office "on the corner of Zumbro and Main Streets. Office hours 11 to 12 A.M., 1 to 4 P.M. and 7 to 8 P.M. Patients will please observe hours as far as possible."

Shortly after St. Mary's opened, considerable feeling was aroused over the state by the alliance of Protestant doctors and Catholic sisters in a hospital enterprise. An attempt was made to boycott the institution and a rival hospital started in Rochester. It soon closed, however, for lack of support. The Mayos and St. Mary's Hospital proved too big to be influenced by obstructing prejudices. They moved ahead, into an era of unprecedented medical success.

CHAPTER TEN

Too Much Money for Two

ROM THE TIME ST. MARY'S
Hospital opened, a considerable portion of its patients required surgical treatment. In the first fifteen months, Doctors
Will and Charlie performed two hundred and nineteen
operations. The nursing problem had to be solved quickly.

To instruct the Franciscan nuns in the technique of caring
for the sick, the hospital engaged Miss Edith Graham, a
graduate nurse with three years' experience in Chicago. She
was a slender and attractive young lady who immediately
won the especial attention of Dr. Charlie. Before the staff
realized it, a romance between the pretty nurse and the rising
young surgeon had started. Dr. Charlie and Miss Graham
were married in April, 1893 at a modest ceremony witnessed
only by the families. They spent a part of their honeymoon

in New York, where Charlie attended postgraduate lectures.

Meantime, St. Mary's prospered with the enlarging practice of the Mayos. The sisters made several improvements in their building in the second year of operation. In the third, the surgeons took time, as did several nuns, to investigate methods of other hospitals. To permit more outside study, the Mayos brought Dr. Augustus White Stinchfield of Eyota to Rochester in 1893 to join them as medical man and diagnostician. He was a person of considerable prominence in southern Minnesota and left a thriving practice to become identified with the Mayos. His specialty was chest work and he directed the use of anesthetics at St. Mary's.

In 1894, St. Mary's engaged its first intern, Dr. Christopher Graham, a brother of Mrs. Charles Mayo. He had been graduated by the University of Minnesota in 1892 as a veterinarian and then studied medicine at the University of Pennsylvania. After joining St. Mary's staff, he relieved the Mayos of their nursing duties. Dr. Graham soon was taken into the Mayo firm, which operated for a few years under the name of "W. W., W. J., C. H. Mayo, A. W. Stinchfield and C. Graham, physicians and surgeons."

As they slowly acquired trusted assistants, the Mayos for nearly thirteen years performed all operations at St. Mary's while maintaining their general practice. The outline of their surgical successes was clearly visible in their initial efforts. It evolved from the development of general surgery in the general practice of medicine until it predominated their clinical work. From that point on, it became the development of surgical specialties within the field of general surgery.

The elder Mayo was forced into pioneer surgery under primitive conditions. He and his sons, before 1889, were typical country doctors with such a large general practice they had little time for surgery. The opening of St. Mary's Hospital changed the picture. It provided Doctors Will and Charlie with more advantageous conditions for surgery than any found elsewhere in the West in a city of Rochester's size.

Both sons possessed remarkable diagnostic intuition. They were strongly inclined from the beginning toward the scalpel, due to their inborn genius, to the knowledge gained from their father and because they were caught by the rising tide of surgery in America. The era in which they started had much to do with their success. New investigations and research were wiping away old methods, old surgical traditions, and baseless beliefs. The medical profession was getting new light. Societies were being formed for mutual protection and enlightenment. Doctors were traveling long distances to study the methods of others. Medical journals were publishing more learned and scientific contributions.

The Mayos were quick to impart to their colleagues the knowledge they gained in the operating room. Dr. Will's first medical paper, read to the Southern Minnesota Medical Association in 1885, was a report of an ovarian-tumor operation. He and his brother contributed more than one thousand papers to medical literature. They were probably surgery's most prolific writers. Neither prepared an article of purely medical interest except from the surgical point of view.

From the first, the Mayos set a standard for the future Mayo Clinic. From 1894 to 1905 they worked only with interns as surgical assistants, initiating practices that later developed into surgical specialties. St. Mary's first report, from September 30, 1889, to January 1, 1893, showed ten hundred and thirty-seven patients were treated at the hospital. In the first three months the Mayos performed fifty-nine operations. The year 1890 saw one hundred and sixty operations and the next two hundred and sixty-one. In this early period, Dr. Will performed forty-seven intra-abdominal operations, revealing his preference and skill in this field. The larger number of eye, skull, and face operations completed by Dr. Charlie in the same period indicated his early development as a proficient "head" doctor.

Dr. Charlie's deftness, as well as originality, in eye, ear, nose, throat, bone, and joint operations was due to a sixth, a mechanical, sense. His versatility astonished observers. No matter what the surgical problem, he quickly mastered it and proceeded without hesitancy. One hour he might be engaged in a cataract or mastoid operation and in the next an excision of a kneejoint. Dr. Charlie's greatest booster was his brother. "Charlie soon had me driven to cover by being a better surgeon," Dr. Will said of that period. "I began to specialize on abdominal work and in operations on the ureters and kidneys."

The doctors astonished the medical fraternity by losing so few of their cases. St. Mary's records reveal success in 98.3 per cent among six hundred and fifty-five operations in the first four years. Such an amazing ratio was rarely equaled elsewhere.

With patients coming from afar to obtain the skilled services of the Mayos, St. Mary's soon was overcrowded. Work on the east wing was started in 1893 and when ready for dedication the following year, Rochester held a civic celebration. Mayor H. H. Witherstine invited the public to inspect the institution, to become better acquainted with it and its nurses. Speeches were delivered by Catholic, Universalist, and Episcopalian clergymen, as well as by the

Doctors Mayo. All trace of the religious dispute of the years before had vanished.

"All success is due to the sisters," Dr. Will remarked. "It was their funds that built and maintained and improved the hospital. We are but the agents of the sisters." Dr. Charlie likewise credited "the success of our work to the constant, skillful care of the sisters."

Meantime, the Old Doctor was enjoying life to the full. He still assisted his sons with operations and called on patients, when he was in Rochester. But Dr. Mayo was now also Senator Mayo and considerable time had to be spent representing his constituents in the state legislature at St. Paul.

There were, also, frequent trips to Chicago, New York, and more distant places to be made in the pursuit of professional knowledge, or pleasure, as the doctor will, and he began to develop a wanderlust that grew with his advancing years. The earnings of the Mayo practice were more than enough to make unnecessary the skimping of his country-doctor days. Doctors Will and Charlie were happy to see their father indulge in the freedoms he had earned by long years of application.

Before the end of 1894, the young doctors took note of a condition that frightened them. They were making too much money! Their homes were paid for. Their offices, which had been enlarged to clinic proportions, were firmly established and profitable. St. Mary's Hospital was filled with their patients. The Mayo medical theories were working out, as indicated by the low mortality rate among their cases.

From the start, the Mayos placed their money in a joint bank account from which each drew funds as needed. They lived out of the same pocketbook, neither asking for nor expecting an accounting from the other. Dr. Will, who kept an expert eye on finances from the first, one day called Dr. Charlie into his office. Checks and banknotes stood heaped on the desk before him.

"Charlie, look at that bunch of money," Will said.

"It's a lot, all right. Quite a wad has come in lately. What are you going to do with all of it?"

"That's what I want to talk to you about. What are we going to do with it?"

"It seems that we've already got more money than any two men have a right to."

"We've got to figure out some use for it, some way to help others."

Dr. Charlie was thoughtful for a moment. "I don't believe our fees are out of line with what other doctors are charging. Of course, there is one way to cut our income. We could reduce our charges, but that will lead to a lot of difficulties."

"Yes, it will. We must consider our profession. We can't pauperize it by cutting our fees. There are thousands of physicians and surgeons who need the income from the standard rates."

"But this question of fees is important. I don't believe all persons should be charged at the same rate."

Dr. Will looked at his brother and a slow smile eased his worried look. "I believe you and I have been thinking along the same lines. I'm convinced we've got to scale our fees in accordance with the patient's means."

"Exactly," Dr. Charlie agreed. "We must give the same treatment to the man without a cent that we give to the millionaire. A man's financial standing should have nothing to do with the treatment he gets. On the other hand, it should have everything to do with what we charge him."

"I'm awfully glad to hear you say that, Charlie. You won't get an argument from me on that issue. What do you figure would be a just way of setting a fee?"

"I haven't made up my mind on that point. What have you thought?"

"What do you say to something like this: We won't charge a man a fee that, knowing his financial condition, he cannot pay inside of a year while meeting all his other normal obligations."

"Why, Will, I'd say offhand that's a pretty fair barometer. It sounds excellent. It's a safe one, I'm sure, because the great majority of patients who can will pay their bills."

"I believe that, too. When a patient leaves us, we'll hand him his bill and if he can pay, he pays. You see that every day. But if he can't pay, there's no more explanation necessary. We're not going to take notes and we're not going to sue anyone for our fees. Men and women are fundamentally too decent and honorable to avoid their obligations and the variations are too rare to give us any concern."

"Well, I guess that takes care of the fee business," Dr. Charlie said. "I don't think anyone will find fault with it. We probably won't get rich on it, but at least it will give the poor fellow who comes here a chance to keep on his feet."

Dr. Will looked out his office window at the long shadows cast by the late summer sun. He resumed the conversation slowly. "Yes, Charlie, that takes care of the fee proposition, but it doesn't solve our problem of what to do with the money that's piling up in the bank. We ought to put that to some good use."

"I'm not much of a fellow to handle money, except spend it, so I guess you'll have to figure out a way, Will. Have you any suggestion?"

"All this money, coming to us from sick folks, some of them downright poor—I just can't look on it as ordinary banknotes, Charlie. There's something different about it, somehow. It's almost holy money, money we should use for a fine and noble purpose."

"Well, all we know is medicine, so maybe we can use it to help the profession and in that way help more sick people."

"Perhaps we could assist young fellows, medical students and doctors just starting out. Help them get a better education, do research and receive advanced training."

"Yes, I think that's it. Take us, for example. We've got four hands for medical treatment and surgery. Now if we had fifty or five hundred hands, we could do a lot more, couldn't we? If we could help a dozen or fifty young fellows to become better doctors, it would be the same as giving us more hands."

"That's the idea, Charlie. Of course, a proposition like that would take a lot of money. We couldn't possibly do it yet, but why couldn't we put aside a part of our income and when it gets big enough find some good way to apply it, such as an endowment to a medical school or create a foundation. I really think we could work out something pretty fine."

"All right, let's look into it," Dr. Charlie said with finality.

Out of the brothers' discussion of their growing fortune came a decision as unique as their philosophy of medical practice and finances. They divided their total wealth, dollar for dollar. One they kept for themselves. The other, their holy money, they gave to an agent for investment, with instructions to apply it to whatever enterprises and activities he considered best.

Their agent was Burt Eaton, a Rochester attorney who had won a reputation among his clients as a shrewd investor. One day Dr. Will called Eaton to his office and tossed at him a bundle of securities the Mayo brothers had purchased with their savings. "For Heaven's sake, take them and see what you can do with the mess," Dr. Will instructed.

Proceeding without an inventory, without a record of interest received or paid, Eaton worked a year to assemble a respectable list of securities. Whenever the Mayo bank account reached $25,000, he appropriated it for investment in more shares and bonds. The Mayos never asked for an accounting, and when Eaton submitted an inventory, it was put aside without comment and forgotten.

It was a day of handsome returns in the Northwest from railroads, from grain, lumber, and mining. Eaton's investments were destined to multiply until they were large enough, in 1915, to finance the Mayo brothers' dream: the Foundation for Medical Education and Research.

Prominent, successful, famous, the Mayos became subjects of widespread newspaper publicity, unwanted and usually objected to by the surgeons. They were sticklers for professional principles, chief of which is unethical advertising. They refused to see reporters, refused to grant interviews to magazine writers, did what they could to discourage public discussion of themselves and their practice.

But like New York City's Empire State Building, the Mayo brothers no longer had need of self-advertisement. Both were too great to be overlooked.

Much of the Mayo "advertising" is traceable to their brother doctors. They came to Rochester from everywhere to stand in awe of the work done in St. Mary's operating rooms. They went away to tell others of it. Grateful patients, cured of their ailments, returned home to spread the good news.

The Mayo habit of speaking the truth, no matter whose ears it burned, cropped out early at medical meetings when the surgeons were in their thirties. Their encounters with outmoded medical beliefs brought them the kind of advertising that has resulted in benefits to all medicine.

CHAPTER ELEVEN

The Mayo Reputation Expands

THE MAYO BROTHERS QUICKLY
recognized the worth of societies and associations of professional men and contributed much to their growth. They
were free in sharing with their colleagues the knowledge
they gained in their varied practice. They co-operated willingly with all who gave promise of advancing medicine.
They refused, however, to follow precedent or acquire habits that violated their simple tastes. For example, they scorned
the elaborate habiliment affected by many of the older doctors. In the late 1800's, beards and sideburns were accepted
marks of the medical man. But not with the Mayos. They
preferred to appear clean-shaven even though it gave them
a boyish appearance, a deadly handicap in the profession. As
a result, the young surgeons frequently were conspicuous

at medical meetings because of their unconventional attire.

Dr. Franklin H. Martin, organizer of the American College of Surgeons, tells of seeing the Mayo "boys" first at a Minnesota Medical Society meeting in 1893. Of Dr. Will he wrote: "A young man modestly stepped forward, was recognized by the presiding officer and began his discussion of a paper that had been presented. His talk was very much to the point and notwithstanding his boyish appearance, his words and manner were most impressive. He did not indulge in the usual complimentary references. The entire audience, including the older wheelhorses of the profession, listened with rapt attention and applauded appreciatively.

"A second young man [Dr. Charlie], a boy in stature and appearance, then addressed the audience. There was a short discussion. An occasional humorous observation brought chuckles from his attentive listeners."

Dr. Martin observed that up-to-date medical articles by the Mayos began to appear in professional journals at this time. He noted the increased interest Rochester held for doctors. He said: "Soon Chicago found adventurous surgeons from the East and Europe tarried a day or two, then traveled on to spend a fortnight in Rochester."

In the early 1890's, Dr. Will achieved further national recognition when he disputed the claims of a high-ranking Army surgeon at an American Medical Association meeting in Atlantic City. The Army man read a paper on cancer, which he illustrated with several charts. He was considered an outstanding authority in surgery, although Dr. Will had performed many hundred more operations than the Army official.

It was the surgeon's theory that cancer was found in "certain places," chiefly in old ones where people had lived for a long time, such as New York, Pennsylvania, and the East generally. "Our studies show that cancer is found in old houses," the Army man declared with finality. "The disease is almost unknown in new regions, like Minnesota, except in the last few years, but it is now becoming prevalent."

When the speaker finished, he was applauded at length. The meeting buzzed with comment, delegates saying to one another, "That's something new on cancer—old houses, old settlements. Maybe he's on the right track."

When the Army officer mentioned Minnesota, Dr. Will took added interest in the address. The speaker was getting into the Mayo bailiwick and he was saying things that did not square with the young surgeon's observations. "Mr. President," Dr. Will called from the floor when the applause subsided. "Mr. President, I would like to comment briefly on the paper just read."

"Doctor—Dr. Mayo, is it? You may have the floor."

Surprised, even hostile, looks were turned on the youthful Minnesotan. He appeared to be only a year or two removed from medical college. What could he add to the authoritative findings of the Army surgeon? He'd merely take up the convention's valuable time, delegates said.

"Mr. President and fellow delegates, I differ with the observations of the last speaker." The glares sharpened. The hall hummed with resentment. Dr. Will had to wait a minute before the audience quieted. "We have just been told that cancer is found chiefly in old places where people have lived a long time and not in new regions, like Minnesota," Dr. Will began. "As some of you may know, I am from

Minnesota and I believe I can, from my observations and experience, speak with some knowledge.

"First, let me say that cancer is a disease of late middle and old age. The incidence of cancer in old communities of the East is quite natural, because there are more older people living there than in the Middle West, and West. As to the theory that cancer thrives in old houses, allow me to point out that old people are quite likely to be living in old dwellings.

"Now, let us consider the comparative absence of cancer in a new region, like Minnesota. Pioneer life requires a vigorous, youthful people and that is why cancer was almost unknown in my state until recently. We are now more settled in the Northwest. We have an older generation. Many of our young people have pushed on to new frontiers, leaving a good percentage of old folks. I am convinced the age of a residence or dwelling has nothing to do with the incidence of cancer. We must look to other causes and recognize that it is a disease of advanced age."

As Dr. Will spoke, the hostile atmosphere cleared. Every delegate listened eagerly. They forgot his youthful appearance and his audacity to dispute an Army medical officer before such an august body of professional men. When he concluded, he was applauded warmly. The presiding officer asked Dr. Will to come to the platform, where he was introduced to the convention's dignitaries.

From that incident, duplicated in later medical association meetings, the name Mayo assumed greater importance and authority. The brothers' operations were being watched by more and more visitors. The accounts these surgeons gave their medical groups provided advertising that could not be ignored, unsolicited as it was by the Mayo establishment.

Many Rochester residents know of some instances where the skill and resourcefulness of the Mayos saved the lowliest of lives. Most, respecting the Mayo dislike for personal glorification, keep their silence. But occasionally a tale sheds light on the surgical philanthropy of the noted brothers.

Julius Reiter, a Farmer-Labor leader who was five times mayor of Rochester, was in the grocery business in 1892 when Dr. Will came to him with a problem. Mr. Reiter had but recently moved to the city.

"In those days, Dr. Will always met every newcomer to Rochester personally," Mr. Reiter said. "I remember shortly after we became acquainted he came to me and asked my help.

"'We have a little German girl from out of town,' Dr. Will told me. 'She is in a serious condition, but we think we can save her life. You can help us if you will find a good German home where this girl can be taken care of while we treat her. She's skin and bones and needs building up.'

"Some weeks before, the little girl had swallowed a lye solution accidentally. The membranes of her throat were seared and the passages closed by adhesions. The Mayos finally obtained permission from her parents to make an opening in her throat and another in her stomach. A small cord was inserted through the closed passage, one end extending from the throat opening, the other from the hole in the stomach. Graduated knots of cord were pulled through the constricted esophagus every few days, until the opening was dilated to normal.

"We took the little girl and her older sister into our home," Mr. Reiter continued. "They lived with us three months. Of course, we received no pay and didn't expect any. I know the Mayos got nothing for their efforts. The girl recovered. She's happily married today and every time I pass through Grand Rapids, Minnesota, I stop to visit her.

"Well, that's an example of how the Mayo name became so well known throughout the Northwest. People talked about cases like that—word-of-mouth advertising, you'd call it."

Even after they attracted men high in the profession to Rochester to watch their work, the Mayos were equally well known in the famous surgical clinics of Chicago and the East. Unannounced, they would turn up to witness the work of the famous Dr. John Benjamin Murphy of Johns Hopkins at Baltimore or attend the lectures of Sir William Osler on abdominal tumors and cancer of the stomach. They were seen as frequently in New York's medical centers, as eager for knowledge as the youngest medical student.

A good deal of the Mayo prominence was engendered by the papers they wrote for professional journals. Doctors wanted to see in action the remarkable fellows they read about. A portion of them came as skeptics, like the editor of the *Annals of Surgery*. When Dr. Will was barely forty years old, he wrote a report about two hundred gall-bladder operations he had performed. It astonished the editor. Determined to find out whether Dr. Will was a liar or a genius, he visited Rochester for personal investigation.

He called at the clinic, inspected St. Mary's, witnessed the Mayos operate. He was quickly convinced. He saw that their establishment and their work not only met the standards of the best Eastern hospitals but in some instances surpassed them.

Two years later, Dr. Will submitted a report on his first thousand gall-bladder cases. The results were so outstanding that groups of medical men started West to observe the

Mayos. Some sent their most difficult cases to Rochester and usually came themselves when in need of surgery. Their best compliment to the Mayos was their comment, "We always bought round-trip tickets."

"I visit Rochester twice a year, to come away each time with a renewed faith in the capacity of our profession and a new inspiration for the work," a well-known physician once remarked.

The growing reliance of medical men on the brothers for their own physical repairs is illustrated by the experience of Dr. A., a prominent New York surgeon who became ill with an internal disorder. After putting a sign on his office door announcing his departure for Europe, he went to Philadelphia to seek the services of a friend, Dr. B. The Philadelphia man was absent. A sign on his door read, "Gone West for a holiday." Dr. A. decided to continue on to Chicago to consult Dr. C., another surgeon friend. When Dr. A. reached Chicago, he learned Dr. C. had gone "South for a vacation."

Perplexed, Dr. A. decided to take his case to the Mayos. On the day he had his operation, he discovered Dr. B. had just left Rochester for Philadelphia and Dr. C. of Chicago was still a patient in a Rochester hospital. Their "vacations" had been spent in the care of the Mayos.

When they were still town-and-country doctors, the brothers divided their practice geographically. Dr. Will called on all patients north and east of Quale's Drugstore in Rochester and Dr. Charlie took the rest. After their work became almost exclusively surgical, they divided their practice anatomically. Dr. Charlie took the territory north of the abdominal diaphragm and south of the pelvis. Dr. Will attended to the vital central region.

How rigidly this became a Mayo rule is shown by the retort Dr. Will made to a man demanding to see the "head" doctor. An officious millionaire arrived in Rochester one morning, brimming with importance and impatience. He bustled from the railroad station to the Clinic and propelled his way into Dr. Will's office.

"Well, well, how do you do? You're a Mayo, aren't you? I want to see the head doctor around here. You're the head doctor, I suppose?"

Dr. Will looked at the millionaire over the top of his spectacles and replied with a modest drawl. "No, I guess you've come to the wrong man. I'm just the belly doctor. It's my brother Charlie you want. He's the head doctor."

As the nineteenth century drew to a close, the Mayo practice had reached the point where the brothers needed surgical assistants. For nearly thirteen years they had done all the operating. Their Clinic was now essentially a well-organized surgical practice. Both had the reputation of being "universal specialists," although Dr. Will was best known for his work on cancer of the stomach and Dr. Charlie for his expertness in goiter and other thyroid operations.

Dr. Melvin C. Millet joined the Mayo staff in 1898 to start a section in urology. Two years later, Dr. Henry S. Plummer came to the Clinic. In 1904, just before the third operating room was opened in St. Mary's Hospital, the Mayos and their assistants performed three thousand one hundred and thirty-one operations. Surgery had assumed such preponderance that only fourteen patients were treated medically that year.

As the need for surgical associates grew, the Mayos trained their own. This policy resulted in the development of a surgical corps with unparalleled unity of standards and ideals. Personal initiative was encouraged. The establishment of laboratories for pathology, post-mortems, surgical, and experimental work, beginning in 1905, greatly facilitated the inquiring spirits among the associates. Soon after, a library and departments of editorial work, art, and photography were organized.

When the east wing of St. Mary's Hospital was finished in 1905 and a third operating room made available, Dr. Edward Starr Judd was put in charge as junior surgeon. Dr. Judd had been Dr. Charlie's aid for two years, and as junior surgeon he remained his first assistant for some time.

Dr. Judd, son of a grain buyer, was a Rochester product. He spent his vacations in the hospital and after being graduated by the University of Minnesota served his internship in St. Mary's. He progressed rapidly and so quickly won a nationwide reputation for unerring skill and judgment that he became an associate surgeon of the Mayos by 1911. When he died on November 30, 1935, at the age of fifty-seven, his fame as a surgical operator was unsurpassed.

Another Mayo associate who helped build the Clinic's reputation was Dr. Emil H. Beckman. He joined the staff as junior surgeon in 1907 and served as assistant to Dr. Will until 1911, when he took charge of St. Mary's Operating Room No. 4 as general surgeon. Dr. Beckman also possessed great skill and uncanny judgment. One day a Scotch surgeon watched him perform a difficult operation. "It was as perfect as a professional's golf," he said. Dr. Beckman died on November 7, 1916.

The third outstanding man to join the Mayo staff was Dr. Donald C. Balfour, who became a junior surgeon of the

Clinic in 1909. Three years later he headed a section of the division of surgery. He made many important contributions in the treatment of stomach disorders.

Honors, which in the years ahead were to be listed by scores, decorated the walls of the Mayo offices and Clinic. Among the first was the presidency of the Minnesota Medical Association, which Dr. Will and later Dr. Charlie filled. Fellowships in learned societies came to both. In 1905 the Royal College of Surgeons of Edinburgh honored Dr. Will, who in the same year was elected president of the American Medical Association. The honorary degrees voted to the Mayos came from colleges and universities of two continents.

The opportunity to travel was sought eagerly by the brothers. Of his wide travels Dr. Will said, "We traveled whenever we thought we could learn something new. I have been across the Atlantic thirty-four times and my brother almost as many times. While one of us was away, we had perfect confidence that the other was carrying on at home."

While the sons were busy at St. Mary's in the spotlight of medical achievement, the older Dr. Mayo was far from idle. He kept a rigid schedule of office hours—11 to 12, 1:30 to 3, 7 to 8—and only emergencies were allowed to interrupt the routine. He maintained his interest in medical societies, retaining his membership in the American Medical Association for nearly fifty years. In his spare time, he wrote papers for professional journals or traveled.

Not until he was eighty years old, in 1899, did he retire from active practice. He traveled much and made two trips around the world in the interest of medical investigation, the last when he was eighty-seven. No one thought him too old for the trip. Two years later he visited some clinics in Mexico. Even in his late years, Dr. Mayo refused to mellow or compromise with his democratic sense. He showed this when he went to England with a crony who had served on the bench in Minnesota. Dr. Mayo and his friend visited a British court and while there the former judge posed in the wig and robes of an English jurist. The gesture so outraged Dr. Mayo that he returned home alone, refusing to travel with a compatriot who aped foreign manners.

After his retirement, Dr. Mayo made daily visits to St. Mary's Hospital. Much of his time, however, was devoted to social calls on old friends and intimates. He continued to have fine horses and rarely went anywhere without them. One day, however, he called on Julius Reiter, his mayor friend. Dr. Mayo was afoot.

"Hello, Doc. What's the matter? Did all your horses break their legs? Why aren't you driving today?"

The old doctor grinned sheepishly. "No, Julius, I'm through driving behind a team. Tomorrow I'm going to start riding in an automobile—my automobile."

"An auto—one of them horseless things? Why, Doc, what's got into you! I never heard anything like it!"

"Yes, the boys don't want me to drive around any more. They bought me an automobile and hired a chauffeur and I'm going to ride around like a big stuffed shirt."

"Well, Doc, I'll swear!"

"Say, Julius, whenever you feel like taking the family out, let me know. I'll give you a ride."

"Say, that's mighty fine! How about next Sunday? My sister's getting married then. Guess we'd look pretty sporty, driving up to the wedding in an automobile."

"Sure you would. I'll bring the machine around."

The next Sunday Dr. Mayo called for the Reiter family and drove them to the ceremony. The doctor spent the afternoon in the garden, telling stories to a crowd of Germans alongside a barrel of beer. "That was one of the best times I can remember," he told Reiter on the way home.

On Dr. Mayo's eighty-fifth birthday, he was honored at a banquet in the Cook Hotel by a hundred well-wishers. When he was ninety, he was still active and hearty and liked to go into the country to tinker with farm machinery. One morning his left hand became caught in a reaper. Before it could be stopped, his arm and hand were mangled.

Taken to the hospital, the old doctor submitted to the first of three operations the injury required. A year after the accident, his hand and forearm were amputated. Severe neuritis set in and the fighting Englishman was finally worn down. He died on March 6, 1911, when almost ninety-two years old.

The death of the elder Mayo was mourned by all Rochester. Schools were closed and business suspended during the hours of the funeral. Soon a movement was started to erect a bronze statue of the pioneer surgeon in one of the city's parks. A monument association was formed to raise funds for the statue. It suggested that citizens leave small contributions at their bank, since no individual would be solicited. Hundreds responded in a few days. Entire school classes marched downtown with their nickels and dimes. In one day, four hundred youngsters called at a bank with their donations.

The bronze likeness stands today in Mayo Park, near the half-million-dollar Mayo Civic Auditorium. Beside it is space waiting for two more statues—those of Dr. Will and Dr.

Charlie. The personality of the little doctor is summed up in the monument's epitaph, which was selected by Dr. Will:

PIONEER: PHYSICIAN: CITIZEN:
A MAN OF HOPE AND FORWARD-LOOKING MIND

Louise Wright Mayo survived her husband by four years, her passing taking place in July 1915, at the age of ninety. Her interest in medicine continued until the last. From the time she was a bride, she read medical journals systematically. When failing strength and eyesight forced her to restrict her reading, she confined herself to articles published by her sons.

Her influence on her husband was necessarily one of helpful restraint. She balanced his impulsive generosity by sound logic and unerring judgment. Her Scotch ancestry made her a woman of strong character and good sense. In the early days, when her husband was away from home, she took his place in caring for the sick. She lived a useful and happy life, ripened to a rich fullness by the achievements of her household.

A few months after Dr. Mayo's death, Rochester was startled again by a new crisis that threatened to take one of the famous brothers. Dr. Charlie, away on a speaking engagement, was reported ill in New York. The word came that death was near.

CHAPTER TWELVE

Surgical Twins Almost Parted

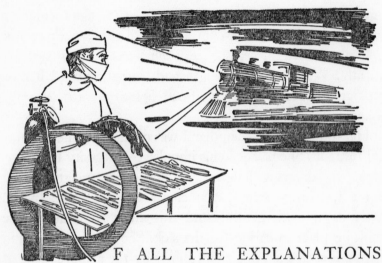

O F ALL THE EXPLANATIONS attempted to account for the success of the Doctors Mayo, perhaps the best is that which emphasizes the brothers' teamwork.

There was a grand canyon of difference in their appearance and personality. Dr. Will was fair, slender, and straight, his face smooth and only slightly lined, his eyes bright and keen but good-humored, his manner brisk but not abrupt. He possessed great driving power, organizing and executive ability. These qualities, together with his militancy, he inherited from the battling Englishman, Father Mayo.

Dr. Charlie was not so tall, not so slender and seemed less masterful than his elder brother. His abundant black hair accentuated his dark complexion. But one, seeing Dr. Charlie for the first time, could focus his attention only on his wonderful dark eyes. In them was the curious look of persons with a delicate sense of touch. In them, too, lurked the mischievous, boyish sense of humor that enlivened everything he did.

Dr. Charlie was the easygoing, inventive, studious, spendthrift member of the Mayo team who most resembled Mother Mayo. He was the congenial mixer and joiner, the jolly good fellow, the orator, the teller of tales, and the master of jokes and pranks. It was Dr. Charlie who drew about him young and old, who had a quip or a wisecrack to illustrate a point and for every occasion.

Two brothers, gifted and skilled, as different as night and day. Yet these dual personalities were as close together as dawn and sunrise. They enjoyed perfect confidence in each other and, as Dr. Christopher Graham, one of their first associates, said, "They are different but they agreed on everything. Either of them would have died for the other."

Appealed to constantly to make speeches to many types of organizations, the Mayos could fill only a part of such requests. "Charlie is the orator in the family," Dr. Will frequently said when asked to make a speech. While he was a practiced speechmaker, he let Dr. Charlie handle much of the platform duties. The younger brother delighted in public appearances and shared his audience's pleasure over jokes and anecdotes interspersing his serious comments.

In a lecture to a medical class, he once startled the students by admonishing them, "Now, mark this date well. In this year the bathtub was introduced west of the Alleghenies. Its use has not yet become epidemic, but it has caused considerable distress on Saturday nights in many quarters."

At a reunion of the Rochester Old Boys and Girls Association, to which the brothers belonged for many years to keep alive their memory of high-school days, Dr. Charlie explained one of his surest means of identifying misty acquaintances. "I don't remember many of the ladies as old schoolmates," he said, "but I may have operated on many of them. So when they stand before me and ask, 'You don't remember me, do you?' I tell them I'm sorry that I don't, but if I could only see their scars. . . ."

Dr. Charlie relished a joke and delighted to play one on the other fellow. He was not above duping a stranger. He was standing once at a soft-drink counter in a Rochester hotel when a visiting Western rancher engaged him in conversation in the easy manner of the small town. The newcomer was a Clinic patient who made much of his ailments and surgical experiences.

Dr. Charlie put on his most innocent look and paid close and sympathetic attention. After an exhaustive account of his infirmities, the Westerner asked abruptly, "Brother, what brings you here?"

Dr. Charlie rolled his eyes in his best lunatic manner. He ran his fingers nervously through his hair. He twitched his shoulders convulsively. With eyes glaring and mouth agape, he gasped, "It's my head!"

The stranger lost no time in backing off and slipping out a side door.

It was the same spirit of good humor that prompted Dr. Charlie to give to Harold Lloyd, the motion-picture comedian, a photograph of himself inscribed, "From one cut-up to another." It seemed natural, too, that he should term a Clinic hallway, filled with glass cases of academic gowns the Mayos had worn at a score of university exercises, the "masquerade room."

In December 1911 Dr. Charlie was in Washington, D.C., to address the Southern Surgical Society. After his talk he felt ill and left for New York to join his wife Edith.

A disturbing telegram came to Dr. Will at Rochester on December 16. It said Dr. Charlie required an emergency operation for acute appendicitis. Dr. Will's first impulse was to speed to his brother's side. But a rigid Mayo rule, which had been laid down years before, required him to remain in Rochester during Dr. Charlie's absence.

Dr. Will phoned to the Presbyterian Hospital in New York and learned his brother had diagnosed his case and had consulted with several doctors about an operation. Dr. Will requested Dr. Joseph A. Blake to perform it. He was reassured some hours later by word that the appendix had been removed and the patient's condition was favorable.

Distressing news came a week later. Mrs. Mayo called Dr. Will early Saturday morning, December 23, and advised him that in the night Dr. Charlie had developed symptoms of acute cholecystitis and inflammation of the gall bladder.

"Oh, Edith, that—that doesn't sound good. Not at all good. What does Dr. Blake say?"

"Will, Charlie's condition is grave. We all recognize that fact here. I'm terribly worried."

"Of course you are, Edith. It shocks me to hear it. I'm coming down there as quickly as I can. I'll come by special train, if I can get one made up."

"But Will, you can't leave home. You know the rule."

"Edith, this is one time the rule doesn't hold. My mind is made up. I will, and I must, leave for New York. I hope to be there Sunday, sooner if possible."

"Thank you, Will. It'll be much better with you here beside Charlie."

The telephone in the dispatcher's office of the Chicago and North Western Railway at Winona rang at 3:58 in the morning. It sounded long and hard, with the ring of urgency.

"Hell—o," drawled the dispatcher.

"This is Dr. Will Mayo at Rochester. I want a special train to take me to New York. When can you have it ready?"

The dispatcher's feet dropped to the floor with a thump and he straightened up in his chair. "A special! Well, let me see. Hold on a minute." A telegraph instrument clattered briefly. "I can fix you up with one from here to Chicago in a few minutes, Dr. Mayo. What you can get out of Chicago I can't say."

"Get yours ready at Winona, then, as quickly as you can."

"How are you going to get over here from Rochester? You're forty-five miles from here, you know."

"Can't you make up something for me? Just one car, or a locomotive? Anything!"

"Wait. I'll see what I can do. I'll call you back in a few minutes."

After what seemed to the anxious doctor a futile eternity, the Winona dispatcher rang back. "Can you ride a switch engine, Dr. Mayo?"

"I can ride anything that runs."

"All right. I got hold of an old switcher over there. They're firing her up right now. If you get down to the station in a few minutes, she'll be ready."

"Thank you. I'll be there."

As Dr. Will turned to switch off the light and leave his office, the door opened and Miss Florence Henderson, Dr. Charlie's special anesthetist, entered carrying an overnight bag.

"Hello Florence! I'm glad you got here so quickly. We're leaving at once. We're going to ride a switch engine to Winona, where we'll catch a special train to Chicago. You're ready, I see."

"Yes, Dr. Will. Let's hurry."

Less than half an hour after his call went through to the Winona dispatcher, Dr. Will climbed into the cab of a dilapidated locomotive streaked with the grime of many hard but useful years. The doctor helped the nurse up the steps. With his hand on the throttle sat A. A. Faes of Waseca, the engineer.

"I'm ready when you are, Doctor," Faes said. "Shall we start?"

"Let her go, sir. And as fast as you can make her run."

With a hiss of steam, the rusty iron horse jerked into life. Displaying the effort and grace of a mastodon, it chugged and rattled across the Rochester railroad yards and headed eastward down the single track to Winona.

Never before had that dingy switch engine gone on such a wild ride. It seemed to shiver in the cold until it warmed to its task. Then it heaved itself over the snow-covered hills, screeched around curves, bumped over crossing frogs, swaying and wavering until it seemed its wheels could never regain the tracks. Acrid smoke, cinders, and biting crystals of snow whirled through the cab and blacked the nerve-taut passengers.

With a whistle of triumph, the switcher charged into Winona at 5:56 o'clock. Before it came to a complete stop, Dr. Will was on the ground, helping Miss Henderson out of the cab. Together they raced across the tracks to a sleek giant of a locomotive, panting in the morning darkness before a single steel car.

With a wave of thanks to the switch-engine crew, Dr. Will scrambled up the steps of his special coach. Almost before he was securely aboard, the train was moving. He glanced at his watch. It was 5:58 A.M.

Ahead, the right of way had been cleared for the Mayo special train. Stopping only for fuel and water, it reached Chicago at 12:35 Saturday afternoon after a record run from Winona. There was a delay. The Christmas traffic had made such heavy demands on the railroads that a special could not be made up for many hours. The Pennsylvania's flier for New York would leave at 2:45 P.M. Dr. Will and the nurse boarded it, resigned to an eighteen-hour trip to the East. They reached New York at 9:40 Sunday morning, December 24.

The record-breaking trip was in vain. Dr. Will reached New York too late for the operation. He was met at the hospital door by Dr. Blake. "We're happy you came so quickly, Dr. Mayo. It was good of you to make such an effort."

"Thank you. How's Charlie? Am I in time to operate?"

"I'm sorry. We had to go ahead. We couldn't possibly wait longer."

"Then you operated? You told him I was coming?"

"Yes, of course."

"How is he?"

"His condition is favorable."

"You did the best thing possible, I'm sure."

"When we saw the symptoms developing, we advised Dr. Charlie of his dangerous condition. He asked that if possible we wait until you arrived."

"He wanted me to operate, didn't he?"

"Yes. But after I consulted with Dr. G. E. Brewer and

Dr. Charles H. Peck, we decided we couldn't put it off longer. We operated at two o'clock yesterday afternoon."

"Mrs. Mayo was with him, no doubt."

"Yes, she held his hand while the anesthetic was administered. I'm satisfied the operation was entirely successful. The patient is in good condition today."

"It's a tremendous relief to hear you say that, Dr. Blake. I'm grateful to you, and to the others. I would like to see Charlie, please."

"Of course."

As Dr. Will entered Dr. Charlie's room, the patient turned his head toward the door. The expectant look in his soft, dark eyes faded into one of happiness and a faint smile turned the corners of his mouth. Dr. Will took his brother's hand and held it a long minute. Words were useless, unnecessary.

Dr. Charlie was slow to regain his health. His brother remained at his side during the Christmas and New Year holidays while the battle for life went on. The physical troubles and sufferings of others must wait for the day when the "surgical twins" could return home, fit to cope with the mounting demands on their skill and talents for healing.

In due time they were back in Rochester, ready and eager to make every contribution possible to medical science. Their rule against leaving their practice simultaneously held true once more, not to be broken again until twenty years passed and another emergency arose.

CHAPTER THIRTEEN

They Picked the Right Parents

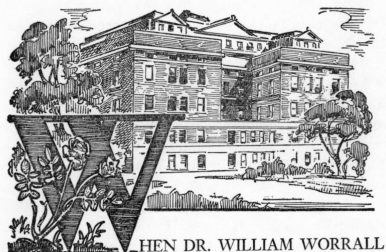

WHEN DR. WILLIAM WORRALL
Mayo first came to Rochester in 1863, he purchased a plot
of ground at the corner of First Street and Second Avenue,
Southwest. There he built his home, an ornamented, ram-
bling dwelling in which Dr. Charlie was born. Forty-nine
years later, in 1912, that site was selected by the Mayo
brothers to house an innovation in medical practice—a clinic
large enough to accommodate fourteen thousand patients a
year. The building, a four-story brick structure, occupied
a quarter of a block and became known as the Mayo Clinic.
Patients and visiting physicians commonly called it that, and
the name stuck.

As work progressed on the Clinic, the citizens of Rochester
watched it with mixed awe and suspicion. It was one of the

largest buildings in the city. Had the Mayos finally over-reached themselves, they wondered? The Mayo practice was large, obviously so, but was it large enough to warrant a whole building on such an elaborate scale? Even the most civic-minded resident asked the question. The Mayos themselves had their doubts.

A short time after the Clinic was completed, Dr. Will and a physician friend drove past in a fast-stepping team of trotters. The friend gazed a bit enviously at the imposing building glistening with newness in the afternoon sunlight. "Dr. Mayo, you have a magnificent plant there for your practice. You should be mighty proud of it and its possibilities."

Dr. Will was silent for a moment. "Yes, I suppose I should be. But I'm wondering whether, in a year or two, they'll be calling it 'Mayos' Folly.'"

At the dedication ceremony, in memory of the elder Mayo, who had devoted himself so ably to human suffering, Dr. Will had declared, "The object of this building is to furnish a permanent home wherein scientific investigation can be made into the causes of diseases that afflict mankind and wherein every effort shall be made to cure the sick and suffering. It is the hope of the founders of this building that in its use the high ideals of the medical profession will always be maintained. Within its walls all classes of people, the poor as well as the rich, without regard to color or creed, shall be cared for without discrimination."

The Clinic became "Mayos' Folly" only in the sense that it was too small, far too small from the very first, to accommodate the thousands who flocked to Rochester to obtain restored health at the hands of the busy surgeons.

By 1913, a year after it opened, twenty-five thousand

persons passed through its offices and laboratories for examination and treatment. Twenty-five thousand patients in a place intended for a maximum of fourteen thousand!

Had some bold spirit of that day predicted a hundred thousand patients would come to a new and larger clinic in a single year, he undoubtedly would have been ridiculed. But that year has arrived. Startling as it is, the Mayo staff has seen the day when one thousand patients registered in a single twenty-four hours. And the limit is not in sight.

What manner of business is this Mayo Clinic? How did it evolve into a streamlined medical workshop?

The Clinic developed in three phases. At first it comprised a group of hospital practitioners caring for patients who came to the Mayos for treatment. When the surgical successes of these practitioners became outstanding, they were forced by the demands made upon them to limit the Clinic's medical work to diagnosis only. There simply wasn't room to do more.

With the enlargement of the establishment into a twenty-two-story edifice, however, the augmented staff, office space, and laboratories made possible the present phase of operation. Now the comprehensive organization provides diagnosis, treatment, hospital management, and convalescence for patients from general and specialty viewpoints in both surgery and medicine.

Behind the efficient functioning of the mammoth medical establishment is, of course, the personality of the Mayos. Their perfect teamwork supplied the motive power, the ideals, the policies that continue to guide the efforts of Rochester's major industry.

What made the Mayo team click? The explanations are many and as varied. Some even attribute their success to the remoteness of their establishment in Rochester, a country town off the trail of commerce, which fired the world's imagination and gave the surgeons a chance to develop free from big-city distractions.

The brothers had their own answer to the secret. Dr. Will once said, "The biggest thing Charlie and I ever did was to pick the father and mother we have. We learned from our father, as a farm boy learns to plow. If we have done much, it was because we were given great opportunities.

"We rode the crest of the first surge of modern medicine. You must not forget, we both had good homes to go to for rest after a trying day."

The elder Mayo, shortly before his death, listed these factors as reasons for his sons' achievements: "Ability, natural and acquired; absolute truthfulness; cleanliness and kindness, even to the poorest. And I taught them that no man is big enough to be independent of others."

There never was a question between the brothers over management of their affairs. Both recognized dominant Dr. Will as the organizer and executive and, as he put it, he "determined things."

Their rights in the Clinic were equal. After the Clinic was established and profitable, they placed themselves and their associates on salaries. The Mayo wages were the same, although each always wanted the other to have the larger share. They never made an accounting to each other until after the Clinic became so large that a formal organization was essential.

In surgery each chose his own field of specialization and gained fame in it. The brothers were quick to grasp the importance of Pasteur's theory of antisepsis, of Lister's application of clinical surgery, of Robert Koch's understanding of germs. These world-famous scientists provided the opportunity which comes but once and the Mayos were ready and intelligent enough to grasp it. Surgery was in transition, from its awkward, fumbling stage to one new, skillful, and clean. The Mayos' first contribution to medicine was to speed the new day.

The Mayo policies, formulated nearly a score of years before, were reiterated with the opening of the Clinic building. Harry J. Harwick, general manager of the Clinic, expressed its financial policy thus: "Just like any professional man does, we try to make our charge fair, according to the service rendered and the financial resources of the patient. If a man is possessed of great wealth, it seems only proper that he should pay more than the man in moderate circumstances. About thirty per cent of our patients pay nothing at all. Another twenty-five per cent pay barely enough to cover the cost of their examination. No fees are accepted from charitable institutions."

Each patient undergoes a physical and financial diagnosis when he registers at the Clinic. There is nothing cold-blooded about the latter examination except that it achieves as nearly as possible absolute fairness and justice to all. As numerous patients have learned, the Clinic has an incredibly accurate method of determining their financial status.

Many are the stories told regarding the fee system the Mayo brothers inaugurated years ago. Among the health pilgrims who walked or hobbled along Rochester's streets—millionaires, movie stars, high officials, capitalists, farmers, merchants, housewives, the poor in spirit and pocketbook—were hundreds who left without leaving a dollar in the Clinic coffers. When their straitened circumstances become known, their bills come to them marked "Paid."

Dr. Will was in his office one day when a woman patient was admitted. She was being discharged as cured after a long period of treatment by Clinic physicians.

"Dr. Mayo, I have come to thank you for the wonderful care I have received," she began haltingly. "I have been cured of my ailment and I shall be eternally grateful to you."

"We are only happy when we can do for all what we have been successful in doing for you. I do appreciate your expression, nevertheless."

"And now, Doctor, may I have my bill?"

Dr. Will looked at the woman from the corner of his eye as he ran through a number of papers on his desk. He noted her pallor and frail shoulders, her thin hands that bore the scars of hard work.

At last he found her account. It included a major operation and weeks of treatment. The regular fee totaled some three hundred dollars. Dr. Will took up a pen and quickly drew a new bill for seventy-five dollars. He handed it to the woman.

"It is most reasonable, Dr. Mayo. But I have only twenty-five dollars. If you will accept that, I promise I will pay the balance just as soon as I can earn it."

Dr. Will nodded slowly. He arose. "Just a moment," he said as he entered an adjoining room. He was back in a minute with two slips of paper. One was a receipt in full for the seventy-five-dollar bill. The other was a check, made payable to the woman, for a like amount.

The other extreme of the Mayo system is illustrated by the experience of a railroad financier, one of the nation's richest men. He was happy over the success of an operation performed on a close relative. To express his pleasure, he sent a large-sized check to the Clinic in payment.

The check was returned at once to the multimillionaire, together with a note informing him "the Mayos usually name their own fees." Three days later he received a bill for three times the amount he considered munificent.

"Preposterous bills" were against the Mayo principles. They never charged more than ten per cent of a patient's annual income.

"That is the maximum," Dr. Will said, "and it does not mean that if a man's income were one hundred thousand dollars a year, we would send him a bill for ten thousand dollars. That would be a preposterous bill." Every dollar of every bill that exceeded one thousand dollars went into a general philanthropic fund.

Sometimes the Mayos accepted payment from a patient only to refund the entire amount when they discovered exceptional sacrifices had been made to pay the bill. This was discovered, to his surprise and delight, by an Iowa farmer who came to the Clinic for an operation.

"What is your source of income?" he was asked.

"I have mortgaged my farm. My crops failed and I had no other means of getting the necessary money."

When the Iowan was ready to return home, he offered a check to pay for his treatment. The Mayos accepted it to prove their good faith. Several days after rejoining his family, the farmer received a letter from the Clinic. With it was his check and one from the Mayos for a like amount. The note explained the money was "a trifling help" toward the loss the farmer had sustained through his illness.

The common folk, who made up the bulk of the horde that descended upon the Mayos, came with unbounded faith in the brothers. "If the Mayos can't fix you up, nobody can," was their almost universal belief.

Many appeared in Rochester with the blessings of their ministers, who frequently gave them penned messages, like the following: "This man has been sick for twenty years. He has saved up enough money to pay for his hospital bill in a last effort to get well. Please help him on his way."

The Mayos permitted no quibbling over charges and fees. They had their standards and they made out their bills accordingly. A Rochester merchant, whose wife had been treated by the Mayos, learned this when he requested a statement of his account.

"I want an itemized account of this bill," the merchant wrote to Dr. Will. "I'm required to do that in my business and I expect it in yours."

"You may be able to itemize calico, but you can't itemize brains," Dr. Will wrote back. The bill was paid without more exchange of correspondence.

While the Clinic commanded most of the Mayos' time and attention, they did not overlook their obligations as residents of Rochester. They were benevolent citizens doing good and correcting evil. About the time the Clinic building was opened, Dr. Charlie took note of a serious public-health situation. He organized a group of women, who stampeded a meeting of the council to demand that steps be taken to change the condition. The councilmen became provoked.

"All right, if Dr. Charlie wants to run things, why doesn't he become health officer?" they asked the women.

Dr. Charlie was informed of the challenge. He accepted it. As Rochester's health officer, he eliminated the trouble. When the duties required too much of his time, he hired a deputy for the job and paid part of his salary from his own pocket. He served as Rochester's health officer 1912 to 1937.

In 1915 Dr. Charlie became a member of the Rochester

school board and remained on it until 1923. For some years he was its vice-president. He was largely instrumental in obtaining up-to-date buildings for the city's pupils. He organized public-health lectures that outdrew the movies. To spread his health program over the entire state, he accepted the presidency of the Minnesota Public Health Association.

Most of Rochester's commerce is geared to serve those who work with or for the Mayo establishment and the two hundred and fifty thousand transients who visit the city annually. The medical center is the magnet that draws this host of visitors. For every Clinic registrant, there is an average of two accompanying visitors. Rarely does a patient come alone. Frequently four and five members of a patient's family are on hand. Latin Americans usually come in large groups, sometimes arriving by airplane or private railroad coach.

Long before the first Clinic building was visioned, the need for more hospital beds was acute. In 1907 John H. Kahler, who operated the Cook Hotel, was asked to form a company to provide extra hospital space. It was the beginning of the Kahler Corporation, which now owns three hotels, three hospitals, a laundry, a dairy company, and a bakery.

While working with and encouraging the corporation to build more hospitals and hotels for their clientele, the Mayos and their Clinic had no financial connection with it. The brothers, until their last years, rarely operated outside St. Mary's Hospital. The Mayo surgical staff today alternates between St. Mary's and the Kahler Corporation hospitals. Unless a patient has a preference, he is assigned to whichever hospital is on his surgeon's operating list.

At five-year periods, St. Mary's Hospital facilities were outgrown. A fairy story of modern medicine was being enacted in a farming town among the rolling hills of southern Minnesota. The three hundred patients of 1890 had increased five years later to six hundred and forty and to twelve hundred and twenty in 1900.

Then began the deluge. Twenty-seven hundred and forty-seven were cared for in 1905 and fifty-four hundred and fifty-seven in 1910. Each new hospital addition was filled promptly. A surgical pavilion with ten operating rooms made St. Mary's the hub of the Clinic's practice. The institution, with nine hundred beds, remains the largest of the independently operated hospitals in Rochester. The eighth addition to the vast plant was opened in the summer of 1941.

Rochester, a city of twenty-eight thousand inhabitants, today lists the astonishing total of thirty-two hundred hospital beds for the sick. Nearly thirty operating rooms are available in the institutions working with the Mayo Clinic.

The Mayos' practice naturally resulted in an impressive bank account. Whereas a score of years before money was a problem, it now made possible the realization of the brothers' ambition. Since their discussion in 1894, the Mayos had set aside half their income for investment. The profits had kept pace with the returns from the Mayo practice, until in 1915 the surgeons were prepared to make their endowment to medical research and education.

A million and a half dollars was in hand for the enterprise. By their brains and skill, their organizing ability and humanitarian pursuits, they had accumulated a fortune. Now they were ready to give it away.

CHAPTER FOURTEEN

They Give Away a Fortune

MEETING, REMINISCENT OF another that took place a score of years before, was in progress in Dr. Will Mayo's office. Its only attendants were the brothers. The subject, again, was money.

"And now, Charlie, let's go over this endowment proposition," Dr. Will was saying. "We've been at this for twenty years, but we've got the money at last. It's time we did something with it."

"Let's see, how much have we? Around a million?"

"A million and a half."

"That's a heap. But you can't say we didn't earn it."

"Oh, you've got to remember much of it is the earnings from investments made with half our income."

"Yes, of course. Well, have you made up your mind

about what you're going to do with that barrel of gold?"

"I guess you've done as much thinking about that as I have, Charlie. We've always figured we'd turn it over to the medical school of the University of Minnesota."

"That money ought to help a lot of students and graduates. We must be sure to protect the principal."

"Naturally. We must stipulate that only the income from the endowment can be expended. The university must agree to hold the endowment intact until it totals two million dollars. Its income will then be sufficient to meet the expenses, which will total one hundred thousand dollars annually. Meantime, we'll have to pay the costs out of our own pockets."

"After the endowment reaches two millions, we can make the Clinic a graduate medical school. As I see it, Will, that should be the real object of this whole proposition— to equip more bright young men to be better doctors, then get them into every country in the world to help the sick."

"That's right. But before a university man can come here to study, he will have his fifth year of work and his B.S. or B.A. degree as well as his M.D."

"What about these fellows coming here to study? They'll need money to live on."

"We'll work out a system of fellowships with salaries so the students can meet their expenses while studying."

"I'm glad you're on the university board of regents, Will, so you can put the proposition to them in the right way," Dr. Charlie said. "The first job is to make clear our motives in this endowment offer."

"I've already sounded out sentiment on the board and I don't believe there is any question but that they will accept it. There may be opposition from other sources, however."

Thus the brothers agreed upon the endowment which became known as the Mayo Foundation for Medical Education and Research. It was formally presented to the University of Minnesota regents at their spring meeting.

Dr. Will had served on the board since 1907, when he was appointed by Governor John A. Johnson, a Democrat. Although he never attended it, he had a great fondness for and interest in the University of Minnesota. He consistently urged that it provide its faculty with the best working conditions and salaries it could afford. He wanted professors and instructors to have more time for travel and study. Although he was a regent until his death, he never accepted a cent of travel allowance. He had the full confidence of other members, who frequently asked, "How does Dr. Mayo stand?" before casting their votes on important issues.

"We, my brother and I, want to turn over to you, the regents of this university, the bulk of our savings of a generation as an outright gift," Dr. Will told the board in explaining the foundation plan. "It shall become the absolute property of the university. We want it to be a continuing fund that will serve the state for generations to come. We realize there will be natural questions as to whether it will work out as we hope. For that reason, I suggest it be given a two-year trial. If, after that time, it is not achieving the results we want, the proposition can be voted out or revised.

"It has long been our dream to give the advantages of our experience and practice to young men. From the early days of the Clinic, volunteer assistants came to Rochester to work with us. We call them Fellows of the Mayo Clinic. They came from the University of Minnesota, from other colleges and universities. You are familiar with such names as these: Dr. E. Starr Judd, Dr. David M. Berkman, Dr. Louis B. Wilson, Dr. Melvin C. Millet, Dr. Henry S. Plummer, Dr. Henry W. Meyerding, Dr. George B. Easterman, and others.

"These are important names, big names, in the medical profession. We wish to associate young and promising men with physicians and surgeons of this caliber. We have no power now to give degrees to Clinic Fellows. By affiliation with the University of Minnesota, the Clinic can train young doctors in advanced fields of medicine and surgery and send them away with degrees, able and skilled practitioners."

The regents promptly approved the plan and negotiations were opened between the Mayos and the university medical faculty for a trial affiliation. They were satisfactory and on June 9, 1915, an agreement was signed.

Opposition to the proposal came from some doctors who saw danger in "merging public with private interests." A bill designed to void the affiliation was introduced in the 1917 session of the state legislature and a public hearing to debate the issue was scheduled in March at the statehouse.

The United States was on the verge of war. Dr. Will's offer to organize a base hospital with doctors and nurses from the Clinic and enlisted men from the University of Minnesota Medical School had just been accepted by the Red Cross.

The hearing took place on a cold, wet spring night. Into the committee room trooped a throng of medical students in trench coats. All available space was taken by speakers and spectators. Dr. Will Mayo sat quietly in a corner, among other physicians and surgeons. His piercing eyes, darting from face to face, betrayed his concern over the outcome of the battle he disliked so heartily. But there was to be no retreat. A life's ambition—the ambition of two men's lives—was at stake.

Among the last to arrive was Senator Henry N. Benson of Nicollet County, chairman of the education committee. He took his place at the head of the table and stood for a minute while the audience quieted. "Before we proceed, I have just one word of caution," Chairman Benson said. "There will be no demonstration, no applause permitted for any speaker. Kindly bear that in mind. We will now hear those in favor of Senate Bill Number 707."

The night of oratory began. For several hours speakers argued for and against the measure. It became late. The committee chairman looked at his watch. "Ladies and gentlemen, we have time for only a few more statements. We have not yet heard from the man most vitally interested in the matter before us. I will therefore call on Dr. Will Mayo to explain his position. Dr. Mayo."

Arising slowly, Dr. Will stood unperturbed but grim. Heads spun toward him. Every eye was focused on his stern face. His black eyebrows were lowered in studied solemnity. Outside, the March wind whipped the rain against the windows. The stillness of the smoke-filled room was broken by the clapping of hands. The applause was taken up by the medical students until it became thunderous.

Dr. George E. Vincent, president of the University of Minnesota, leaped to his feet to quiet the demonstration. He looked at the committee chairman, then sat down quickly. Flabbergasted, he saw Senator Benson, who had warned against any acclamation, leading the applause.

Dr. Will stood unsmiling, waiting for the audience to be still. "Mr. Chairman, ladies and gentlemen: I do not want to keep you much longer. But I am glad to have this opportunity to state publicly the position of my brother and myself on the question of the Mayo Foundation and its connection with the University of Minnesota. In all our endeavors we have been guided by ideals. When the first hospital was built in this country, it was almost on the level with poorhouses and jails. It was difficult to get people to go to one. Well, my father did a great deal to dispel that prejudice. And out of his determination to do it was born the ideal that my brother and I like to think we are living up to in honor of him and of medicine.

"We like to think that perhaps we could provide one place on God's green earth where a sick man of middle income is as well treated as the sick rich man and the sick pauper. And so my brother and I set up the ideal that everyone who came into our Clinic and hung up his hat was to get treatment regardless of the cost and no one was asked if he had the price. We wanted all who came to us to be clothed only in the nakedness of his distress.

"What we are doing is no more than any doctor is doing. You know the kind of man your doctor is and you know he isn't suing people. You know, too, he does a large amount of charity work because the medical profession is altruistic."

Dr. Will paused. He observed a softening on the cold faces of the physicians and surgeons who had spoken before him. He turned his attention again to the committee members, huddled about their table in close attention.

"From 1894 onward my brother and I have never used more than half our income on ourselves and our families; lately, much less. The other half of our earnings was set aside. It became holy money to us. That holy money had to go back into the service of the humanity that had paid it to us. And so we decided on a means of taking up the medical and surgical education of selected and promising men where the state leaves off. My interest and my brother's interest is to train men for the service of humanity.

"What can I do with one pair of hands? If I can train fifty or five hundred pairs, I have helped hand on the torch. We concluded the best way to do this was to create the Mayo Foundation for Medical Education and Research and to turn it over to the University of Minnesota as a trust fund. The plan has been in operation two years. The fund now totals two million dollars and the income from that sum pays its expenses.

"The Foundation provides fellowships at Rochester for advanced study and training of university graduates. It provides funds for the study of epidemics and for medical research. The Mayo Foundation is the absolute property of the university and it is governed by the board of regents. It shares in the income of the Mayo Clinic.

"That is the kind of proposition to which a good many of you are opposed. Why? Is our method of business wrong? We have never taken notes at the Clinic. No mortgage has ever been given on a home to pay a bill there. We never sue. People will tell you that my brother and I own all those hotels in Rochester and make a big profit from them. We never had one dollar's worth of interest in those hotels or any other business enterprise at any time, have not now and never will."

The speaker paused again and ran his handkerchief across his brow. He took a long breath. The audience sat immovable, waiting for his next words.

"I can't understand why this opposition to the affiliation should be raised. It seems the idea of some persons that ne one can want to do something for anybody without having a sinister motive back of it. If we wanted money, we have it. That can't be the reason for our offer. We want to serve the state that has given us so much and we think the best way we can serve it is through medical education.

"I don't give two raps whether the medical profession of the state likes the way this money has been offered. It wasn't their money. My brother and I are over fifty years old. We feel this money belongs to the two and one-half million people of the state.

"What better can we do than devote our remaining years to the work? There's a line in Lincoln's Gettysburg Address that explains why we want to do this: 'That these dead shall not have died in vain.' "

Dr. Will sat down. A moment of silence was broken by a burst of applause that lasted several minutes. It seemed to clear the air, for that night and for the years ahead. Opposition to the Mayo Foundation was over.

Today few if any of those who saw grave peril in the affiliation do not agree that the Foundation has placed the medical school of the state of Minnesota high among the nation's best. The dispute over the affiliation was submerged almost at once by a far graver issue. Two weeks after the hearing on the bill, the United States declared war against Germany and her allies. Medical science, as well as military and industrial forces of the nation, was mobilized to its new task.

CHAPTER FIFTEEN

Mayos Serve Their Country in War

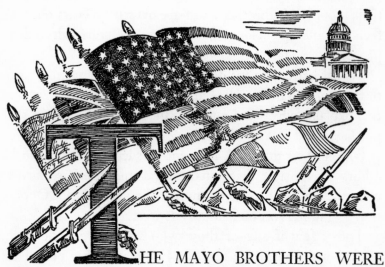

HE MAYO BROTHERS WERE among the outstanding men of the nation who gave their time and skill to the job of winning the war.

When their services were required by their country, they were ready for the call. Even before World War I, they held commissions in the United States Army. In 1912 Dr. Will was made a first lieutenant in the medical reserve corps. Dr. Charlie was given a similar commission the next year.

With the outbreak of hostilities between the United States and Germany on April 6, 1917, the Mayos were among the first officers summoned. Three days after war began, the surgeons were notified they had been commissioned majors in the medical reserve corps. They were needed in Washington by Surgeon General William Crawford Gorgas. How soon could they report?

The brothers faced a problem. They wanted to perform Army duties, yet there were scores of patients under their care in Rochester. Should their long-standing rule—never to leave the city simultaneously—be shelved in the interest of the national emergency? Tackling the issue without delay, the brothers worked out a plan that not only satisfied the Army chiefs, but proved of great benefit to the entire military medical force.

It was decided that one of the Mayos would be on active duty in Washington for six months, while the other remained at home. There he not only looked after the Clinic's business, but conducted a postgraduate training center for the Army and Navy medical corps, giving service doctors expert instruction in surgery and treatment of wounded soldiers and sailors.

Alternating for six-month periods between home and Washington, they served as chief consultants for the surgical service. Dr. Charlie assisted in co-ordinating the work of the government's welfare and health bureaus and divisions. He also was named a member of the advisory committee to Brigadier General C. E. Sawyer.

The Rochester postgraduate training center quickly assumed such importance that the Army instructed Clinic staff members not to enroll in the uniformed service. Many, however, were eager for military duty. The insistent ones enlisted and were sent overseas, where they performed brilliant medical, surgical, and pathological work. Dr. Charlie helped to organize a base hospital unit that went to France.

Dr. Charlie especially would hardly have passed muster at West Point for military decorum. It meant little or nothing to him. He wore a uniform because regulations called for one, but its snap and style were of no consequence. What he found much more intriguing was reorganization of the Army's medical department.

Dr. Franklin H. Martin tells of meeting Dr. Charlie strolling down Washington's Pennsylvania Avenue shortly after he was commissioned a major. It was a warm day, so Dr. Charlie had his uniform coat unbuttoned—violation number one of military etiquette. He wore only one boot spur because he had misplaced the other. That one was upside down. When a passing private saluted him, he appeared surprised.

His lackadaisical attitude toward his honor was a source of worry to Charles Mayo, Junior. The boy was walking with his father one day when men in uniform passed constantly and saluted the major. After a time Dr. Charlie tired of raising and lowering his arm. Frequently he "forgot" to acknowledge the salute. Whenever he failed to return the courtesy, he was checked up by his son, who warned, "Pop, you missed another!"

Both Dr. Will and Dr. Charlie took their Army duties very seriously. As members of the Army medical board, they rarely missed meetings at Washington. Their suggestions were of such value that the Army reorganized its medical department on the basis of the Mayo recommendations.

On July 15, 1918, the surgeons were made colonels in the medical corps of the U. S. Army. When a doctor friend saw Dr. Charlie wearing his colonel's eagle for the first time, he offered congratulations. They were received with as much embarrassment as a bride shows over comment on her wedding ring. Although they were honored and feted as were few scientific men, the Mayos never heard words spoken in their praise without being utterly abashed.

The brothers were in active service until February 20, 1919, when they were assigned again to the medical reserve. They were rewarded that year with the Distinguished Service Medal and commissioned brigadier generals in the medical corps. Later the French and Italian governments paid them military honors.

Dr. Charlie never did grow accustomed to his military titles. After he became a brigadier general on November 22, 1921, in the Medical Officers' Reserve Corps, he was asked to address the military cadets of Carlisle University. As he approached the campus, escorted by a friend in a car bearing the brigadier general's flag, he heard the booming of cannon.

"Listen to that!" Dr. Charlie exclaimed. "They're having artillery practice today. That's fine! I can watch them shoot."

The escort looked at the surgeon with some surprise. "I'm afraid you're going to be disappointed, Dr. Mayo. That shooting happens to be the thirteen-gun salute in your honor."

Even at home Dr. Charlie couldn't escape the embarrassments of his position. A party of distinguished English medical men, on a wartime survey of America, stopped at Rochester and were overnight guests of Dr. Charlie. As was customary on retiring, they placed their shoes outside their bedroom doors for polishing.

Dr. Charlie, the last to go to bed, noticed with some misgivings the row of footwear. The demands of war had almost depleted his servant staff. It was too late at night to call in assistance. There was only one thing to do. He took the shoes, a pair at a time, to the kitchen and spent half the night polishing them.

The Mayos' Army connections were maintained even after the age limit automatically caused their retirement. They were commissioned brigadier generals in the Auxiliary Medical Reserve Corps and held that rank through their last years. Dr. Charlie until his death was consultant in surgery in the office of the surgeon general, assigned to serve in case of emergency.

Military officers detailed to the special postgraduate training center at the Mayo Clinic always received a warm welcome from the brothers, who made every facility available to them. The Clinic for years conducted a fortnight of inactive duty training for officers of the medical reserve corps of both Army and Navy.

The Mayos were good friends of soldiers and former service men. They were charter members of the William T. McCoy American Legion Post of Rochester and provided it with a permanent home in the Mayo Civic Auditorium. They often expressed their happiness in aiding the Legion to conduct its work on behalf of community, state, and nation. The twenty-three bell carillon atop the Mayo Clinic tower was purchased by the brothers in England and dedicated in 1928 to the American soldier.

The demands of war over and the Foundation operating successfully, the Mayos sought a means to perpetuate the educational and research efforts they had endowed. Late in 1919 they organized the Mayo Properties Association, which became a philanthropic trustee of all the wealth possessed by the Clinic. Thus on January 1, 1920, the association was incorporated to facilitate use of the Clinic properties. To it was deeded all real estate—of which it has considerable in Rochester—records, equipment, materials, securities, personal property and the like, owned and used in connection with the Mayo Clinic, the income of which must forever be devoted to educational and research pursuits.

Under the Mayo plan, there is no division of Clinic profits. All doctors and workers are on salary and any surplus after salaries and expenses are paid is diverted to the Properties Association as rent for use of the Clinic building.

A board of nine Clinic officials and professional staff members governs the Properties Association. It is their duty to protect the Mayo Foundation for Medical Education and Research by the proper handling of the association income. The system of management was not left to chance by the Mayos, however.

"My brother and I could not be sure that any plan of administration we had worked out would be feasible forever," Dr. Will said after its organization. "How can we be sure what will be the wisest way a hundred years from now, or a hundred and fifty, or even fifty? So it is provided that if the present plan ever proves not feasible, the whole plant goes over to the University of Minnesota to be administered by it, just as it now administers the Mayo Foundation, which has been its absolute property since 1915.

"The very roof of my home goes out of the possession of my family when I die. It is already turned over to the Foundation. I wouldn't want my children to be deprived of the fun and the benefit of wanting something and going out and fighting to get it. And I think, from the rich men with whom I have talked, that this idea has penetrated far more deeply into American life than many imagine."

In the final twenty years of their lives, the Mayos were

motivated by a great social vision—medical education and research. At their suggestion ten per cent of the Foundation's income yearly is expended outside Minnesota and another ten per cent is used to investigate epidemics both within and outside the state. In furtherance of their vision, the Mayos made the Clinic the only one of its kind enlisted in the cause of training new doctors for all the world.

One consuming desire guided the Mayos in their efforts. They sought perfect work. It became an ideal: The best, and that only. The brothers had a great advantage over their confreres in large cities. At no time were they tempted, or even permitted, to become specialists. From the beginning of their practice every kind of ailment came to them and they had the opportunity to examine, diagnose, and treat them all. Precedents did not fetter them. They were simple men, untiring in their labors to find new truths and to throw off old habits.

To eliminate diagnostic errors, the Mayos built a staff of the best men obtainable. They enlisted expert radiologists, clinicians, pathologists, physiologists, chemists, and laboratory men for their institution. These men investigated and studied, and when their reports were ready, they turned them over to the Mayos, who made the final decisions. The treatment alone called for the Mayos' personal attention.

A patient was not left in doubt as to the ultimate development of his ailment. The Mayos early won a reputation for absolute honesty with their clients. They never hesitated to turn down any case they thought they could not benefit. Such frankness won for them unexampled confidence.

Even when their authority had been established, when they no longer had theories to prove or statistics to expand, they kept giving to the world all the information their work was capable of demonstrating. The complete medical record of every patient who entered the Clinic was maintained in an elaborate catalogue system, even after he or she left Rochester.

Much thought was given to the patient, from the cab fare charged him to ride from the station to the Clinic, his hospital or hotel, to the strictest economy in his treatment. Patients were urged to leave hospitals at the earliest moment, to obtain less expensive quarters in nursing homes which abound in Rochester.

The Mayos from the beginning were clever men. Their unlimited experience and unusual ability gave them boldness of execution. Yet in all they did there was a naturalness and earnestness that came from the desire to do the best they could to benefit others. Self-seeking had no part in their make-up and their results demonstrated it.

Late in the 1920's the Mayos were again faced with an acute problem. For many years their Clinic building had proved itself too cramped. Now the pressure was becoming so great that the staff was hopelessly handicapped.

St. Mary's Hospital in 1920 alone had cared for seventy-four hundred and thirty-five patients and in 1925 had treated eighty-three hundred and ninety-six. The other institutions were likewise crowded. The surgical staff performed twenty-two thousand, seven hundred operations in 1920 and the following years saw the number increased steadily.

"Charlie, we've got to have a larger Clinic building. We need more elbow room," Dr. Will said to his brother at one of their frequent personal conferences. "We've got to build again."

"Well, let's make it big enough this time. We might as well put up a skyscraper and really put a gang of doctors to work. Folks will probably think we're crazy, but I'm tired of being packed in here like a sardine. We need about four or five times the room we now have."

"Yes, we do. The number coming here is growing too fast for us under existing conditions. We'd better get some architects busy and see what they can do."

The result was the present three-million-dollar building, three hundred feet tall, towering above Rochester's skyline like a beacon of hope and cheer to the thousands who came for the ministry of the Mayos.

CHAPTER SIXTEEN

A Twenty-two-Story Doctors' Office

IN THE CENTER OF ROCHES-
ter, Minnesota, around which the community of twenty-
eight thousand inhabitants literally revolves, stands a splendid
limestone, brick, and terra-cotta edifice topped by a pillared
tower. It is the city's tallest and largest structure, an office
building that has the dignity of a cathedral. It is one of the
strangest buildings in the world, for within its thirteen main
floors it houses a private medical practice owned by a philanthropic association.

It is known today in every land as the Mayo Clinic, founded
by the three Doctors Mayo on the principle that every man
has a right to the best in medical advice and practice, regardless of his ability to pay for that service.

The three-million-dollar structure, which was opened in April 1929, overshadows an adjoining four-story brick building. Few persons, when visiting Rochester or the Clinic for the first time, are even aware of it. Yet it is the original Mayo Clinic building, which in 1914 Dr. Will feared might become known as "Mayos' Folly." The skyscraper beside it dwarfs it completely.

The visitor entering the Clinic building gains the impression that he has stepped into a metropolitan hotel lobby. A throng of patients, their families or companions move across the wide corridor to the right toward a battery of elevators or to the left toward the administration offices and general waiting room. Doors ajar along the hallways give one a glimpse of busy office workers, stacks of filing cabinets, desks and typewriters. This mixture of clerical and medical efficiency seems bizarre until one remembers that this is a big business plant whose real estate and equipment are worth no one will say how many millions.

To staff this mammoth Clinic, between four and five hundred doctors and some twelve hundred other workers are on the payroll. After the modern Clinic building was completed in 1929 and there finally was room for the expansion they desired, the Mayos induced the most competent men they could find to become their associates. The fact that they were able to gather nearly five hundred experts from the world's most highly individualistic profession to come to a small Middle Western town, far from any metropolis, to live and work and be content, speaks volumes for the high regard the profession held for them. Especially after the World War, the Mayos added to the Clinic faculty many educators and investigators.

The Clinic is democratic in its rule. Each staff member of

five years' standing is given one vote in the business sessions of the organization. What salaries are paid the associates remains a close secret of the Clinic, but if one hazards the guess that the fourteen general surgeons probably are paid fifty thousand dollars each annually, the answer in Rochester is likely to be, "I wouldn't be surprised." Besides his salary, each staff member has the benefits of a pension and insurance plan. He makes at least one inspection trip a year.

Under operation of the Mayo Foundation, the Clinic serves as the postgraduate school of the University of Minnesota Medical School. After medical students have completed their fifth year of work and have their doctor of medicine degree, they are eligible for one of the hundred and eighty-four Clinic fellowships.

Each Fellow studies three years at Rochester and is paid a sum considered enough to maintain himself comfortably. The first year he receives six hundred dollars, the second seven hundred and fifty dollars, and nine hundred dollars the third. A Fellow studies and does research under the direction of Clinic staff members who are also on the faculty of the graduate school. Fellowships are so highly prized that fifteen hundred doctors apply for the sixty to seventy available annually.

Mayo Fellows are not confined to the University of Minnesota. They come from all over the world—Uruguay and Iceland, Cape Town and London, Hawaii and Australia. Of more than fifteen hundred men and women who studied in the Mayo Foundation, more than five hundred are in medical schools in the United States and abroad.

"If a medical man can come and show he's got the stuff in him, we won't shut the door in his face," Dr. Will said after the postgraduate school was established. "Homeopaths and all, we shut the door of learning to nobody. What we are doing at the Clinic looks big because it is done in mass. That is the only difference with what is being done by the profession in other places. I am satisfied that what we are doing here can be done in other places. The advantage of doing this work in mass is that the patient gets the benefit of all the resources.

"Occasionally a staff member comes to us with a proposition that costs money and asks, 'Can I do that?' I tell him, 'You can do anything you think you ought to do with a sick man's money.' My brother and I are merely trustees of such funds. The purpose of the Clinic is not to take sick folks' money, but to take care of sick folks. But not to pauperize them. We haven't a charity bed—not one. The whole institution rests on mankind's sense of moral obligation and at the same time it functions along the lines of sane, fair business administration.

"I believe the same kind of proposition can be made to function in the same way elsewhere. By that I mean not to foster paupers, but at the same time to benefit suffering people."

The patient who came to the Clinic for the first time registered at the main desk, was given a number and then waited. Waiting was likely to be one of his chief occupations in the examination period—waiting in line to see the physician to whom he was assigned, or waiting in the lobby auditorium. He had to cultivate patience until called.

Except in emergency or when he carried a prized ticket reading "Friend of Dr. Mayo," the patient could do little to get preferred attention. For the system did not allow for half measures.

As Dr. Will put it, "Instead of the patient having one spoke looked over, we go over the whole wheel."

Nothing was left to chance or speculation. By the time the patient had gone through the mill of office consultations, laboratory examinations, check-ups and the rest of the Clinic routine, his life—past, present, and probably future—was charted, indexed, and catalogued so that there was little chance for professional error.

Frequently, after the patient had finished his examination, he would be given the diagnosis of his ailment and told that a certain physician in his home city could perform the operation or give the necessary treatment. The choice was left to the patient. More than likely he would decide to have the work done by a member of the Clinic or one of the Mayos, but many were persuaded it was to their economic interest to go back home for care or surgery. And just as well.

While the Mayos and their Clinic won their reputation on miracles of surgery, less than one-third of all patients who went to Rochester had operations. Often the fear that surgery was necessary was quickly dispelled by a Clinic examination. The Mayos were outspoken in telling a client when no operation was needed. They likewise were as open in revealing when there was no hope for cure in any type of treatment.

The doctors' workday began at seven o'clock each morning. Almost without exception, the scene was St. Mary's Hospital. A spirit of peacefulness ruled the institution. Posted in the operating amphitheaters were the day's lists of surgical jobs, often twenty, sometimes more, and of all varieties. The chief surgeons had their tasks lightened somewhat by the consultations each patient had at the Clinic with a dozen assistants—physicians and specialists—who studied every case and made their diagnosis. Only the final decision was left to one or the other Mayo.

Promptly at eight o'clock the first patients, anesthetized by a skilled nurse, were wheeled into the rooms where Dr. Will and Dr. Charlie stood ready. With skill and dexterity they applied the scalpel. Their work was almost bloodless and immaculate.

One observer described them at work thus: "They applied the best methods of every great surgeon with a deliberateness and sureness which seemed devoid of haste. Yet they worked with marvelous rapidity. Once having begun an operation, none of the doctors ever hesitated until it was completed and the wound sewed. They accomplished in fifteen minutes what no other surgeon in the world could do in less than an hour."

As soon as the operations were completed, the rooms were cleaned with damp cloths and the next anesthetized patients brought in. In this brief interval, the Mayos rested for a few minutes on a bed in an adjoining room.

When each operation began, a bell notified medical spectators who passed at will from one operating room to the other to watch the surgeons at work. The visitors, in shirt sleeves, occupied tiers of movable seats. As many as thirty or forty doctors witnessed most operations. A privileged few stood beside the operating surgeon. They were required to wear white sleeveless frocks, which effectively prevented them from touching instruments or the patient.

Thus the daily routine went on without interruption until noon or one o'clock. Dr. Will devoted himself mainly to abdominal surgery, especially the liver, stomach, the gall bladder, and intestines. Dr. Charlie's program included operations varying between cataracts, clubfeet, hernia, and goiter.

The approximate time for each operation was determined in advance by the surgeons. Thus each patient was under the influence of the anesthetic for a minimum period.

The practice of welcoming spectators to their operating rooms was decided upon by the Mayos when they first searched for medical knowledge. "When we were very young men, we made it a point to go any place where we thought we could learn something to improve our surgery," Dr. Will explained. "When we would get to the operating room, they would let us in, but they always seemed to have a lot of tall assistants with orders to stand in such a way that we could see little or nothing. I told Charlie that if we ever had anything worth showing, we would make it easy for any visitor to see what was going on."

As early as 1900 surgeons flocked to Rochester to avail themselves of the opportunity to see the Mayos in action. Sometimes as many as fifty were in the room at one time. Perched high on their movable seats, they had unobstructed views. This treatment of visitors had much to do with spreading the fame of the doctors.

The Mayos developed a system of laboratories that greatly facilitated their work. Beside the operating theater was a pathological test room. The instant the case under treatment furnished a piece of tissue for diagnosis, a bell summoned the attending pathologist, who could tell, while the patient was still on the operating table, whether a tumor was malignant or not. In this search for the causes of cancer, Dr. Louis B. Wilson and Dr. William Carpenter McCarthy were especially valuable to the Mayos.

The workmanship of the Mayos brought forth many expressions of admiration from surgeons who watched them. The late Dr. Arthur A. Law once said, "They take too many portrait pictures of Dr. Will. What should be perpetuated for the good of surgery is a movie of his hands doing a delicate operation."

Fred B. Snyder, chairman of the board of regents of the University of Minnesota, asked Dr. Will once what made him an outstanding surgeon.

"Perhaps it is because I am endowed with the faculty to decide, and the skill to execute, at the crisis of an operation hard to do, how far I can go to save a life," he replied.

While the Mayos were credited with originality in their operations and surgical techniques, they made no exaggerated claims. Dr. Will frequently remarked to his audience, when applying a suture in an unusual manner, that "this is the Hippocrates-Mayo suture." His listeners would at once understand it was his way of claiming priority in its use, but at the same time suggesting it may have been employed originally by the Father of Medicine or someone even earlier.

The Mayos' many contributions to medical literature were written because they believed that in the study and preparation of an article the writer gained more than did the reader. When time permitted, they extended their critical observation of surgery in other clinics in America and abroad. For many years, Dr. Will wrote a travelogue from his notes and impressions of his trips. He attributed to these clinical excursions much of his success and progress in surgery. The brothers were extremely regular and systematic in their habits, in their scientific reading as well as in their clinical work.

"One's contribution to the art and science of surgery

cannot be measured by those which are original," Dr. Will said in discussing claims to fame based on initial practices. "For that matter, many things which are thought to be original have been previously discovered and forgotten, so that many so-called discoveries are really rediscoveries. Those of importance of which I might speak, the following, as far as I know, were original with me.

"At the meeting of the surgical section of the American Medical Association in 1903, I brought out the overlapping—from above down or from side to side—method of repair of umbilical and postoperative abdominal hernias. The radical cure of these hernias up to that time had seldom been accomplished and this easy and simple method has now been adopted all over the world. I was first to advise removal of gall bladders from below up, which has now been generally adopted, and the first to describe and practice implantation of the hepatic duct or stump of an injured common duct in the duodenum when there was irreparable damage to the common duct.

"With Doctors Wilson and Griffin I wrote a paper on acquired diverticulitis of the large intestine, which I read at the meeting of the American Surgical Association in 1907, the first time this condition had been demonstrated in the living and operated upon directly. I also advocated the transabdominal sigmoidectomy for removal of pedunculated papillomas and other similar growths of the sigmoid. I was the first to give careful description of the proximal half of the large intestine in its anatomy and lymphatic distribution in relation to the excision of the right half of the colon.

"In a paper on hyperplastic tuberculosis of the intestinal tract, I made the first detailed description in American literature, as far as I know, of cases in which presence of the condition was proved at operation, with recovery of the patient after removal. Concerning the kidney and ureter, I first described the method for reattachment of the ureter to the pelvis and methods of removal of the diseased half of the horseshoe kidney, with a report of cases. I first described removal of ureteral stones suprapubic extraperitoneal cystotomy and incision of the lower ureter. I also demonstrated a simple method of anastomosis of the two ends of the *vas deferens* after it had been injured or divided."

Some authorities consider Dr. Will's method of treating cancer of the stomach his outstanding contribution to surgery. His radical operations for this type of tumor were the first and his procedure was applied in thousands of Clinic cases. He was also noted for his operations on ulcers of the stomach and duodenum. Ironically, just such an ailment caused his death.

Even when Dr. Will could be prodded into discussing the surgical procedures he created, he invariably concluded his remarks by saying, "My brother has made more original contributions than I have."

Dr. Charlie not only was a wizard with the scalpel, but he possessed an inventive bent that advanced his profession. He devised a dissecting scissors that became standard twenty-five years ago. The operating table he made for the original St. Mary's Hospital was widely copied. He was recognized as the originator of modern goiter surgery and likewise was a pioneer in the surgical treatment of the nervous system. He first used the "Mayo operation" for varicose veins, a technique utilized for thirty years until supplanted by injection treatment.

Dr. Charlie's method of operating on bunions became general and he devised new ways to treat brain, throat, ear and nose ailments. In his late years he became interested in plastic surgery. The operations he performed in his fifty years of practice total uncounted thousands.

In fifteen eventful years, years of the ascendancy of surgery, the Mayo brothers established themselves as the "modern miracle workers." Their reputation was made quickly and the whole world knew of their professional standing.

But the human side of the Mayos, their simplicity, their interest in their fellow men, their desire to escape the spotlight of fame, was slower to come to the fore. Its revelation increases the stature of the brothers as men belonging to and having a great regard for the common folk.

CHAPTER SEVENTEEN

What the Mayo Brothers Were Like

HEN CHARLIE GETS SO BUSY on his farm that he forgets to have his shoes cleaned, he takes a night sleeper to Chicago, knowing that he will find them well polished under his berth in the morning," Dr. Will once remarked jokingly in hinting at his brother's disregard for the value of money. Yet it told much about the likable and good-humored younger brother. He took more pride in his three-thousand-acre farm, Mayowood, than in any other visible evidence of his success. When a stranger on a train asked him what his occupation was, he replied, "A Minnesota farmer."

It was characteristic of Dr. Will to answer the same question by saying he was "C. H. Mayo's elder brother." There was a powerful bond between the two. Each knew the other's strengths and weaknesses. Both recognized Dr. Will's business acumen and Dr. Charlie's winning ways with individuals and crowds. Together they made an unbeatable team and together they worked harmoniously, eager always that the other should have the greater portion of wealth, fame, honor, and success. Each gave the other credit for their achievements; jealousies never existed between them.

Even the newcomer, meeting the Mayos for the first time, quickly appropriated the universal titles of "Dr. Will" and "Dr. Charlie" when speaking to or about the surgeons. To the brothers there was only one Dr. Mayo—their father, the country doctor of Le Sueur.

The Mayo Clinic staff referred to Dr. Will as "The Chief." His brother was simply "Dr. Charlie." The difference in titles is a reliable clue to the position each held in the estimation of their colleagues.

Dr. Will paid the price of being at the top. As chief of the Clinic, he was the administrator, the organizer, and the disciplinarian. He was a man of intense determination. When he set out for some objective, he achieved it if within human realization. There were times when the wheels he set in motion caught men clinging to positions dangerous to them. If they clung too long, the centrifugal force of his efforts threw them off and they were hurt.

The difference in personalities of the brothers was reflected in the reaction of patients at the Clinic. Dr. Charlie would leave his private office and step into a waiting room. Two or three women, having waited for hours, would rise and approach the doctor. Their attitudes bespoke supplication. Seeking a chance to be heard, they hovered about, watching eagerly, reaching out shyly to touch his hand or arm.

Half an hour later Dr. Will might leave his office and appear in the same room. His austerity balked even the thought of liberties some patients took with the younger brother.

Dr. Will held high social ideals and felt keenly the responsibility of his obligations to less fortunate men. Yet he seldom unbent professionally and his manner was coldly impersonal. He scorned the "bedside manner" and left to his brother any coddling of the sick.

"There is no place for emotionalism in medicine," he said, "because sympathy is a luxury a doctor can ill afford."

The brothers never hesitated publicly to express their high regard for each other. Dr. Charlie admired the business ability of Dr. Will and always allowed him to take the lead in joint business affairs. "Will can't make a mistake," he frequently said.

Dr. Will paid one of his finest compliments to his brother on the observance of his seventieth birthday. He addressed a Mayo Clinic staff meeting and announced his retirement from executive authority. "It is time for me to pass on to the next generation," he said. Then turning to a topic on which he was always eloquent, he continued, "Something more than four years younger, Charlie has stimulated me by precept and example, and our association has been unique not only in the love and confidence we have for each other, but in having made an opportunity for two men to work as one and to share equally such rewards as have come.

"With due regard to the statement of the truth, Charles H. Mayo is not only the best clinical surgeon I have ever known, but he has that essential attribute of the true gentleman—consideration for others."

At another time, when the citizens of Rochester were

honoring Dr. Charlie after his election in 1916 to the presidency of the American Medical Association, Dr. Will expressed his high opinion of his brother.

"When I was fourteen and Charlie ten, father gave us a job hoeing some corn," Dr. Will related. "We had some trouble solving what we would do with the money we earned. Finally under Charlie's able leadership, we purchased a steam engine. Charlie became the engineer and after a time I was promoted to the honorable job of fireman. I never did understand that engine and didn't understand how Charlie made it go. But he did, and he is still making things go.

"He is a most prolific and original being. The president of the American Medical Association is selected on well-defined lines. He cannot be a candidate for the office, but must have produced a large volume of medical writings and medical progress. And these my brother Charlie has done. As to original contributions, no man has produced more. He is an inspiring teacher and makes the average man want to work. I consider Charlie the greatest living surgeon."

Some eleven years before, Dr. Will had been similarly honored by the American Medical Association. He was then forty-four, the organization's youngest president. As guest of Rochester citizens, he was given a silver loving cup. In his speech of acceptance, he claimed equal distinction for his brother. "Together we have labored side by side and the achievements of one are achievements of the other," he said.

Besides their interest in medicine, the Mayos were men of wide general knowledge and understanding. Their travels gave them an international outlook. They were as frank in pointing to evils in political or social life as they were in their own field. Lay as well as professional groups listened to their advice and opinions on secular topics.

On the question of liquor, Dr. Will cautioned physicians especially against its use. As late as 1934 he wrote in the staff bulletin of the Mayo Clinic that from his medical observations, drinking had nothing in its favor and a very great deal to condemn it. "As doctors, we must begin to think of promoting the cause of temperance," he wrote. "How often do we hear, when we are speaking of a certain man, 'A very bright man, but he drinks.' Of my classmates in college, so far as I know, none of those who drank steadily are now living and of those who were addicts to even a very mild degree, from the time the addiction became manifest, none progressed or maintained his position. One of the greatest surgeons in the world told me he had never known a surgeon of the first rank who was in the habit of using alcoholic drink."

The liquor question must be looked upon impartially, without connecting it with prohibition or personal liberty, Dr. Will urged. "The medical men are many whose memories go back to the time, not only of the corner saloon but of several more saloons in the middle of the block," he went on. "There the American citizen who so desired could stop to spend his money and drink the shoes and stockings off his children's feet and then go home to beat his wife. This was called an expression of personal liberty. My idea in bringing this matter to younger minds is to see whether you cannot get at some answer to the alcohol question, which has seemed up to the present time to have aroused only sound and fury and controversy."

While he himself did not smoke, Dr. Will did not disapprove of the practice, even for women. In speaking to a group of social workers in Rochester, he said women had as much right as men to the practice. He went on to say that many things have come into life in recent years to add to the happiness of individuals, and in doing so have brought longer life.

The Mayos were born Episcopalians and were members of the Church but, as Dr. Will said, never "worked at it much." Despite the fact that he had not attended services of his church in twenty years, he considered himself fundamentally a religious man and was a stout defender of religion's efficacy as an aid to medicine.

"The emotions of a man play an important part in the practice of medicine and religion deals with emotions," he said. "I know there are many to whom I cannot demonstrate the existence of God and the human soul as I can demonstrate some point in surgery to a class. But in my own heart I know there is a God and I know there is a human soul. Call it by any name you want, there is something in humanity that is above and beyond any material calculation of science.

"The world needs religion. It needs religion as distinguished from creeds born of theologians' disputes. The surgeon and physician realize quickly that they need religion to help them. I do not mean the personal religion of the surgeon and physician—I mean the personal religion of the patient. I have seen patients that were dead by all medical standards. We knew they could not live. But I have seen a minister come to the bedside of that patient and do something for that patient I could not do, although I had done everything in my professional power. But something touched some immortal spark in him and, in defiance of medical knowledge and materialistic common sense, he lived.

"Religion is the universal comforter in times of physical or spiritual distress. Let us not delude ourselves into believing that Communism or the state can take the place of some form of spiritual belief. There is a tendency for a group of intellectuals—persons who have been educated beyond their intelligence—to underrate the value of religion as the universal comforter, but to the mass of people, religion has the same potency it has had for two thousand years. No thinking, reverent man can read the Sermon on the Mount or the life of Christ without knowing here is truth."

The Mayos were good citizens of Rochester who gave of their personal funds that the townsfolk might better enjoy their city. Two of Rochester's parks are gifts of the brothers. Always interested in music, they provided means for public concerts and built a music pavilion in one park. On summer nights artists from the Minneapolis Symphony Orchestra were brought to Rochester, and the Mayos paid part of the expenses.

Dr. Charlie's enjoyment of music was so keen that he installed a pipe organ in his home and learned to play it well when more than fifty years old.

One of the last benefactions the brothers bestowed upon Rochester was the gift of the attractive Mayo Civic Auditorium, built at a cost of four hundred and fifty thousand dollars.

Dr. Will, despite his wide fame, was determined to be no different from the home folks. His dislike for being pointed out by patients and visitors as a local celebrity prevented him from being seen often on the city's streets. Yet he maintained old friendships and was loyal to them. To keep alive the memories of his high-school years, he maintained his membership in the Rochester Old Boys and Girls Association. His friends delighted to recall that Dr. Will, as a boy, was termed a "tease" by the girls.

Not the least of the Mayo achievements was their ability

to keep fit and on the job despite prodigious duties and demands on their time. For years on end they were at work from seven o'clock in the morning until five o'clock in the afternoon, often later. Many an evening was taken up with meetings of Clinic staff members.

A routine so strenuous would probably be too much for a city man, subject to the distractions and pace of metropolitan life. The Mayos, besides finding joy and happiness in their profession, knew how to relax. They found the secret to a pattern of life that kept them hale and eager for the next day's adventures. Both had big, comfortable homes where their family life was most congenial. The doors were open at all times to friends. Except on special occasions, the doctors were abed by curfew time.

Asked how he found energy to accomplish as much as he did, Dr. Charlie replied, "If a man is interested in his work, he finds the strength for it in the working of the old proverb, which says, 'The back of the ass is shaped to the burden.'"

Like most successful men, the Mayos early developed hobbies which became important parts of their activities. Dr. Charlie liked golf, but his inherent interest was in the land, which he turned into the development of his magnificent farm, Mayowood.

Here he built a large home on a high knoll overlooking the rolling hills, meadows, and woods of the estate. To make it easily accessible to his office, he constructed a motor road that permitted him to reach the Clinic in twenty minutes. He had the Zumbro River dammed to form an artificial lake, which he stocked with wildfowl, and bought deer and elk to roam through the wooded acres. He developed excellent herds of Holstein and Guernsey cattle, which stood high on the prize list of Olmsted County for milk and butterfat production.

On his farm, Dr. Charlie had a large hothouse which he glazed with X ray plates instead of ordinary glass. Whenever he took his guests there, he always watched with a sly expression their looks of amazement as they saw outlined against the sky the bones and intestines of anonymous Clinic patients.

Dr. Charlie loved Mayowood, and its cost was little concern of his. This disregard for expense is best illustrated by a story he told of his experience with agricultural experts he hired to operate the farm.

"The first year I hired an expert and he wasn't much good," he related. "I lost fifty thousand dollars. The next year I got a better man and I lost only twenty-five thousand dollars. And then I got a wonderful expert. He ran the farm for the third year—and I lost only fifteen thousand."

Dr. Charlie liked to talk with and to farmers and he sometimes addressed groups of them from his own county. "The farm is still a good place to live on and eighty per cent of the farmers are doing well," he said in 1933. "These farmers have been careful of their machinery and buildings and did not get themselves into debt when times were better and money easy to obtain. There are sixteen million acres of land that used to raise hay, oats, and corn to feed horses, which have been supplemented by autos and tractors. It is no wonder that there is a surplus of these crops."

While Dr. Charlie was a born farmer, his brother had an especial dislike for rural life. When the boys were young, their father purchased a farm inside Rochester's city limits. Will would have nothing to do with it. Charlie's love for the land was derived from his mother. He remained always a bluff, kindly farm doctor who spoke of tumors "as large as turnips" and "goiters like ears of corn shedding their husks."

Dr. Will sought recreation in motoring and on the water. To satisfy his need of rest, he and Mrs. Mayo planned a river boat embodying their nautical tastes. Their ideas were incorporated in the *North Star*, a luxurious yacht launched at St. Paul in the summer of 1922. It was a one-hundred-and-twenty-foot pleasure craft, constructed at a cost of thirty-five thousand dollars. It was the largest screw-propelled vessel on the river at the time and was fitted with every comfort for the Mayos and their guests.

To this yacht, usually berthed at Winona, Minnesota, Dr. Will went for his summer week ends to rest, to write medical papers, to talk with friends about ways to improve and expand medicine. Cruising leisurely along the Mississippi, the *North Star* provided the surgeon and his family with the seclusion denied them in busy Rochester. It became his club, his refuge from work and care.

Gathering about him the friends he liked and those he thought would enjoy a boatride, Dr. Will turned the craft over to their fancy. There was no schedule except for meals. Liquor was not allowed aboard. If a guest went to the upper deck and stayed alone for half a day, he was not considered queer. If another preferred to read, or sit and watch the scenery, or take a nap, the host encouraged him to do so. Dr. Will was an ardent believer in the siesta and practiced it himself for many years.

He was always ready to talk about medicine, hospitals, and the findings of his colleagues. Not because medicine was an obsession. For him, there was nothing of equal interest. It was his source of happiness and service. He was a man in love with his profession.

Usually a secretary was aboard for the week end cruise, and Dr. Will spent much time writing papers for medical meetings. County medical societies met on the *North Star* annually. Graduating classes of Rochester nurses and convalescent Clinic staff members were entertained on the yacht. Each year the craft was run to Minneapolis and the regents of the University of Minnesota taken for a trip.

But in 1938 there was no meeting of the regents on the *North Star*. Dr. Will announced that he and his wife had decided to sell it. He could no longer enjoy it because "it made me feel conspicuous when so many people are poor." The yacht was purchased by General T. Q. Ashburn, president of the Inland Waterways Corporation, for inspection purposes. Dr. Will used the proceeds for a charitable enterprise.

Dr. Will's other hobby, to which he gave much time, was travel. He especially liked to motor. "I can sit still and rest if the thing I am sitting in is moving," he said.

He was devoted to his wife and two daughters, Carrie and Phoebe. Three of the Mayo daughters died in infancy. To intimates, the couple was always "Will and Hattie." Mrs. Mayo, the surgeon's favorite companion, was dignified, calm, and self-contained. She is credited with being responsible for a good measure of her husband's success. She made Dr. Will's home life free of worries, so that he could devote his full energies to his profession. Carrie married Dr. Donald C. Balfour, a director of the Mayo Foundation, and Phoebe is the wife of Dr. Waltman Walters, a prominent Clinic surgeon.

Dr. Will abstained from the use of both tobacco and alcohol. Golf, cards, and detective stories were likewise scorned as means of relaxation. He found that in the study of medicine. "We never had cocktails in our home," he said. "We never drank nor smoked. It is tremendously important not to set a bad example for young people. However, anything which gives us pleasure and does not harm us physically is a good thing."

One of the lesser-known hobbies of Dr. Will was his interest in boxing. While a student at the University of Michigan, he was a prize-winning boxer at one hundred and twenty-seven pounds. He attended many professional fights, but was rarely recognized because of his desire to keep out of the limelight. He witnessed the heavyweight championship fight in Chicago between Jack Dempsey and Gene Tunney, made famous by the "long count" against the champion. He believed that incident a great mistake and resented it strongly. Aside from Dr. Will's interest in boxing, neither brother cared for sports.

Usually thought of as austere and sober, Dr. Will, when surrounded by persons he knew well, enjoyed a facetious moment. He made an inspection trip one time with the board of regents to the university's Grand Rapids Experiment Station. A study was being made of muskeg land for farming purposes. Much money had been spent on it, with little results.

"I suggest that a concrete floor be laid over the muskeg and covered with plenty of good soil to make sure of a good crop," Dr. Will said with a grin.

One of Dr. Will's last acts, with approval of his wife, was to give their large home and extensive gardens, "with an endowment sufficient for their maintenance, to the purposes of the Mayo Foundation." The donors "hoped" the home would be turned into a meeting place where men of medicine could exchange ideas for the good of mankind.

The Will Mayo home is now known as the Foundation House, a club for Fellows of the Foundation and professional visitors. Near by, Dr. Will built a smaller dwelling, from where he could see the Foundation House put to the use he and his wife intended for it.

Dr. Charlie's home life was similar to his brother's. There he found rest and the surcease from the worries and strain of his labors. He had a family of eight children, two of whom died when young. Dorothy was the oldest child and lived at home. Next was Dr. Charles W., who is now a Clinic surgeon. A daughter, Edith, married Dr. Fred W. Rankin of Lexington, Kentucky. Dr. Joseph G. Mayo, Dr. Charlie's second son, was on the road to becoming an important figure in the Clinic when he was accidentally killed in 1936. The other children are Louise, wife of George Trenholm of Rochester, and Esther, wife of John Hartzell of Detroit. Dr. Charlie's household also included two adopted children, John and Marilyn. The large family's behavior was quite informal, in keeping with the spirit of the head of the house. One time, son Joseph came home from school with a companion. He greeted his father by saying, "Hey, Pop, where's the key to your music box"—referring to Dr. Charlie's pipe organ. "Here's a fellow who can really play it."

Dr. Charlie's sons were brought up to continue the family medical tradition. Joseph from the first evinced interest in medicine, in preference to surgery, and when he entered the Clinic he devoted himself to this field. His elder brother, Charles, however, showed an aptitude for surgery and, when thirty-two years old, became a Clinic surgeon in his own right.

Dr. Charlie made no public pronouncements of his views on drinking and smoking. Whatever his indulgence in stimulants or tobacco, they took place if at all in strict privacy.

The harmony in the brothers' family lives was a natural reflection of the amity that marked their personal relations. They had based all brotherly dealings on a mutual confidence in the other's high motives and ideals. One never started an important work or a new venture without first asking the opinion of the other.

The lives of the Mayo brothers provide an excellent pattern for the regulation of democratic institutions. They sought wealth, frankly and openly, but only to help others and not for the transient glory of being rich. Their preference was for a simple, not an ornate, life.

CHAPTER EIGHTEEN

The Doctors Speak

THE MAYO METHODS WERE far from hidebound. They freely sought information on new techniques in surgery and as freely offered to others the results of their research and discoveries. It early became a policy of the Mayo Clinic that no important medical meeting at home or abroad should be without a Mayo representative. As a result of their co-operative spirit, medical men came to Rochester from all over the world.

Both surgeons traveled to almost every land to contact outstanding physicians and technicians. As many as they could, they brought to Rochester to help advance the Clinic's work. There was no regard for cost. Europe knew Rochester well as a great medical center. A good proportion of the three thousand surgeons who appeared at the Clinic each year to study came from abroad.

"No surgeon in France has completed his education until he visits Rochester," a French medical expert said. "The Mayos are kings of Rochester. They are also its benefactors."

Long before most professional men considered themselves more than established in their local field, the Mayos had assumed unquestioned medical leadership. In the two score years of their surgical practice, they accepted the presidency of every important national body in the field of medicine. They applied a blend of skill and a compelling drive toward perfection. Their talents, combined with a prodigious ability to work, carried them to heights undreamed of by doctors of the fumbling medical era the Mayos helped to end.

From their knowledge of mankind, gained through treating the diseased and suffering, the Mayos held a deep respect for human beings. They sympathized with their aspirations, with the yearnings of the mass for religion and education and the desire for self-improvement.

They gave time and money freely to bring to more persons the essentials for human happiness. Each individual, no matter what his station, was worthy of the best effort of doctor and educator, the Mayos believed. And on that premise they anchored their philosophy of personal and professional conduct.

Dr. Will, especially, was endowed strongly with the characteristic of foresight. He was among the first to recognize the worth of Pasteur's and Lister's discoveries. He saw immediately that their application opened a wholly new field to clinical scientists.

Surgery, he saw, had need to be established on a higher ethical level. To attain that goal, he believed surgeons needed laboratories and scientists to help them. The medical clinic itself needed an ally. That aid was the proper connection with an educational institution in order to provide rising young doctors with valuable clinical training. When that idea proved too advanced for many colleagues, he fought for it until he had convinced them he was right. Dr. Will, as a dominating personality, impressed all with his great capacity for accomplishing things.

"He would have been a success in anything," a former associate said. "If it hadn't been surgery, he'd have been another Ford, or a senator, or maybe President of the United States."

The idea that either or both of the Mayos would make excellent government executives was advanced seriously on several occasions. One time, Frank A. Day, a Minnesota country editor of considerable prominence, started a boom for Dr. Will for governor of Minnesota. The response was electric and a campaign was about to be organized. Dr. Will was out of the state at the time. When he heard of it, he lost no time in returning and squelching the plan.

In 1920 S. D. Van Meter of Denver, a prominent Colorado Democrat, proposed to Minnesotans that Dr. Will be backed as a Presidential candidate at the San Francisco convention. The enthusiastic Mr. Van Meter said, "In the person of Dr. William J. Mayo of Rochester you have, first, a proved executive; second, a real Democrat; third, a genial, friend-making diplomat; fourth, a wealthy, independent man who is a big-hearted friend of the working poor; fifth, a man who is known in every hamlet and crossroad post office through the local doctor; sixth, a man that no public honor can turn his head, having already made himself the greatest surgical success in the history of the world." Dr.

Will again discouraged the boomlet and it vanished in the haze of political oratory and manipulation.

But still another attempt was made to bring the surgeon into the political arena. In 1927 Dr. R. S. Hill of Montgomery, Alabama, challenged "the country to find a flaw in his [Dr. Will's] qualifications and fitness" to be President. "Dr. Mayo is a man whose natural gifts fit him for a foremost position in any department of human endeavor," Dr. Hill said. "He is free from suspicion of alliance with any corrupt, selfish interests; a believer in law enforcement and a big man, one who will command universal respect and confidence. As a President he would be a superb executive, moved and controlled by naught but the single purpose of great and righteous achievements."

Dr. Charlie in 1924 was likewise suggested as candidate for the Presidency, but he, like his brother, had neither the time nor inclination to enter politics. He laughed down all attempts to interest him in a fight for votes. "I never had time enough in all my life to conduct a campaign," Dr. Charlie said. "My profession requires almost every minute at my disposal."

Medicine, and medicine alone, commanded their unswerving attention. Each new day was likely to produce an adventure in some uncharted medical or surgical field. The older they became, the more convinced were they that great unexplored areas remained for the scientific man.

When they were in medical college they heard learned professors say, in all seriousness, "We are done with medicine; we've got the whole thing." With this prudent observation the Mayos disagreed. They returned home to prove its falsity.

"So many things are on the way now that people think

of medicine as something new," Dr. Charlie one time remarked. "Thirty or forty years ago professors told us we knew the whole of medicine. But we shall never have the whole thing. Medicine is like a hallway lined with doors, each door opening into a different room and each room opening into another hallway, again lined with doors. Medicine is always wonderful and will never be finished."

American medical science had in Dr. Charlie one of its stanchest defenders. In an address delivered in New York, he declared, "Many important American discoveries in medicine have not been accepted here until they have been appropriated by the Germans and returned to us with the stamp, 'Made in Germany.'"

He belittled the "gland treatment" craze of the 1920's as "mostly humorous." He urged newspapers to devote less space to "freak surgical and medical performances." When asked about rejuvenation, he asked, "Who wants to live twice? I don't know much about the thing, but I hope it doesn't work. After a man passes seventy, the brain begins to slow up. Nobody has succeeded in eliminating old age. A lot of people think aloud and sometimes their thoughts transplanted to paper are accepted as facts."

Dr. Will and Dr. Charlie knew their limitations and did not fight old age. They retired from surgical practice when sixty-six and relinquished all executive authority when they reached seventy. They retained, however, their wisdom gained from study and experience and used their last years to guide others and to counsel younger men in clinic and research organization.

Recent medical progress is based largely on diagnosis and early treatment, Dr. Will said in the middle 1930's. "We used to see people only after they were dead. Now we get an opportunity to treat them as cases. Early diagnosis, early treatment, early surgery, prevent cases from reaching the hopeless stage."

Changes are as sure to come in medicine as in other lines of endeavor, Dr. Charlie predicted. "Diseases change, as man is brought into contact with new conditions—intellectual, social, and so on. What might be good treatment in my generation, when the patient was confronted with certain environmental conditions, might not be a good treatment now. As conditions change, medicine must change with them."

Both Dr. Will and Dr. Charlie looked forward to the time when the average expectancy of life will attain the Biblical three score and ten. In an address before the South Dakota Medical Association, Dr. Will asserted, "The next generation probably will reach the full three score and ten of Biblical days." He attributed longer life expectancy to the advances in medicine and better habits of living.

Despite the higher toll of automobile accidents and the increase in smoking and drinking among Americans, the Federal Census Bureau determined in 1941 that the average life span had reached 62.5 years, an increase of 3.3 years over the previous decade.

"Since the close of the Civil War, approximately twenty years have been added to the average length of human life," Dr. Will pointed out. "Medicine in the World War was triumphant. For the first time in the history of wars, the number of deaths from casualties was greater than the number of deaths from disease. In the Spanish-American War, one man died of gunshot wounds to thirty who died of disease."

Dr. Will probably devoted more time to the study of cancer than to any other disease. He startled the medical world with his radical operations for removal of malignant tumors. He became an authority who pioneered the way in its treatment. Despite the deadliness of cancer, he was highly optimistic over the prospect of finding the causes and providing the cures. He believed the day was coming when most persons susceptible to the ailment would be made immune by increasing their resistance to it.

"Ten per cent of the people of later life die of cancer," he said in an address to a group of prominent Minneapolis residents. "I don't think it is an accident that some have it and others do not. I think they lack resistance to the disease. I believe we will be able to increase the resistance of that ten per cent so they won't have it."

Dr. Will found that thirty per cent of cancers are in the stomach and that heat was a source of irritation. "Food too hot to be borne comfortably in the mouth should not be taken into the stomach," he warned.

Overindulgence in food was rebuked on numerous occasions by the doctors. Dr. Charlie told the Rotary International in 1937, "Counting the cost of the chemical elements in our make-up, our bodies are worth ninety-eight cents. Too many of us are putting four-dollar meals into those ninety-eight-cent bodies. Most of us nowadays are eating not wisely but too well. We are living to eat rather than eating to live. Most of us eat too much and many eat too much of some food materials and not enough of others."

As an additional warning he said, "In an operation, a fat man is three times the risk of a lean one. People think too much about their health, but not too much if they would think intelligently. Good health rests with the individual who must learn to take care of his health early in life."

Dr. Charlie studied for many years the effects of focal

infection and had an important part in creating the co-
operative relations between dentistry and medicine. In pointing out that eighty-seven per cent of all deaths in the United
States are caused by an infection of some sort, he alluded
to this link between preventive medicine and dentistry in
an address before the American Dental Association. He
added that the mouth is the source of sixty per cent of the
diseases resulting from infection.

"Preventive medicine today, in so far as older adults are
concerned, revolves around attempts to determine at the
earliest possible moment presence of signs, not only in order
that happy, useful life may be prolonged, but that we may
grow old gracefully and free as possible from debility and
incapacity," he said.

"To live happily, when retired, we must develop earlier
in life an avocation to maintain our interest in life. Such
outside lines of thought and diversion are the more successful
when they bring us in contact with nature—birds, gardens,
geology, and the like. Trying to be happy by means of jazz
is about as vain and unsatisfactory as trying to make a meal
out of pickles and pepper. It does not afford durable enjoyment. The very tempo of jazz is feverish, exciting and con-
ducive to the wrong pace for American life. It is sadly out
of date. We need a new tempo."

The increase in insanity in the United States was a cause
of much concern to the Mayos. Dr. Charlie, in pointing out
that the number of insane persons doubled in thirty years,
traced the cause to the large number of immigrants who
were not assimilated into the scheme of American living.

"The world has moved ahead so fast in material civilization that man has almost got behind in his power of
adaptation," Dr. Charlie told the American College of Sur-

geons. "Every other hospital bed in the United States is for mentally afflicted, insane, idiotic, feeble-minded and senile persons. There is an enormous number who are almost fit for the asylum.

"Many people live in an age when they are dependent and senile. Only five per cent of our people, at the age of sixty-five, have independent incomes. I would rather die when my brain fails than to live on."

Dr. Will noted that mental distress of the depression era of the 1930's caused most of the increase in brain ailments. "The growth of insanity cases has become a matter of grave concern because of the public expense and the increasing efforts required to protect the public from insane people," he remarked. "It is as important to cure the economic evils which burden humanity and cause insanity as it is to apply remedies to individual cases."

What about the field of medical practice? Is it becoming overcrowded? Are the opportunities as great as ever?

To the question of educating young doctors, the Mayos gave much time, thought, and money. They endowed the Mayo Foundation to increase the opportunities for bright and hard-working medical-school graduates. But they found many things wrong with the educational system that produced doctors.

"We are trying to turn out specialists and all-around scientists wholesale in our medical schools and we are merely burning up a lot of young men. It can't be done," Dr. Will told a group of Mayo Clinic physicians. "Medicine is apt to become an aristocratic profession, so stiff is the expense and so long the course. I believe we must come to a time when all higher specialties will be taught in the graduate departments.

"Heads of medical schools should think twice before giving prizes to leading students, because those in the rear are liable to be just as good. Let us graduate from our schools a good garden variety of doctors and then take those who have vision and spirit and put them in the graduate schools. The idea of taking all students and making them all specialists has gone too far.

"Forty years ago we had too many 'family doctors.' Now we have too few. General practice is now having to depend upon the older generation. Medicine needs recruits. We need country doctors. The difficulty lies in the matter of training. Its high cost in time and money is making the profession aristocratic and eliminating the man of modest means. That is all wrong and shouldn't be so.

"I believe there should be a reduction in the time requirements that would lessen the time spent in preparation and thereby cut the cost. One, probably two, years could be taken out of grammar and high-school courses. There is no reason why students entering medical school, at their best in mental and physical activities, should not be able to work the year around and finish their medical course in three years.

"The long period of from two to four years in the university before the student begins his medical course dulls his mind. Why should these young people at the strongest period of life continue in the educational system of the grammar school? The young doctor should be in practice before he is thirty years old."

The importance the Mayos attached to education in the program for public health is reflected in Dr. Charlie's remarks to the Minnesota Public Health Association in 1933. "Great medical discoveries do not cure people of disease," he said. "They provide only the essential knowledge and

tools. The problem of public education waits when the
scientist is through. One of the greatest advances in American civilization is the health movement which has swept the
country in recent years.

"We must either educate the people or dictate. The public
is in a difficult position. With the radio blaring out cancer
cures sponsored by someone without an hour's medical education, even while reputable physicians are also speaking
over the air, the average man is apt to be confused. The
public should find out who is sponsoring the speakers. A
large part of this education over the radio is in the hands of
irresponsible people."

The brothers were never satisfied with their knowledge of
medicine. Although famous and even when nearing the close
of their remarkable careers, they declared they had much
to learn.

Every new development aroused their interest. If they
could not go in person to observe it, they sent out young
physicians from the Clinic. Any progress in the treatment
of cancer was sought especially. The information gained by
the Clinic representatives was brought back to Rochester for
examination, experiment, and application.

When Dr. Will laid down the scalpel after he was sixty-
six, he did so because he realized he was no longer fully in
tune with the rising generation of medical men. "I observed
younger men, really possessed in the enthusiasm of youth,
had the ability to grasp and orient new knowledge even
though it conflicted with their experience—an ability I no
longer had in so marked a degree," he explained. "I had the
wisdom of experience, but I also carried the weight of past
responsibilities."

Then in a reflective mood he added, "To be frank about

it, we have accomplished much, my brother and I. But we should have done great things. We were given the opportunity. We were born at the right time and to the right parents. Perhaps no one will ever again have the opportunity to accomplish so much. That day is gone, unless for some genius. We were not geniuses. We were only hard workers. We were reared in medicine, like a farmer boy is reared in farming."

After abandoning the operating room, Dr. Will remained a Clinic consultant until he reached seventy. In this capacity he found one of the greatest joys of life—sitting back and watching life go by. "Younger men are going up the ladder while older ones are coming down," he observed. "It is only right that the older men aid as they pass. Each generation must take care of its own affairs. The general rule that a man should retire from an executive position at seventy is well founded. Try as he will, the experiences of the past are clearer to him than his thoughts of the future. His knowledge is static."

However, a man of seventy need not consider himself on the shelf, Dr. Charlie insisted. "If a man has gained something through his lifework, so that the next generation will go to him for advice, that is right and proper. But to retain the power to compel them to accept his advice is not good. If a man has trouble in his joints at any age, he knows it; when his head doesn't work well, everyone else knows it, but he probably won't. The younger and the older must travel together. The young have the imagination, the old the experience. So it must be with medical science."

Determined as they were not to enter politics, the Mayos frequently pointed to the perils they saw in the path of democracy. Dr. Charlie, after his retirement, gave much thought to our political system. He summed his philosophy in a commencement address he delivered in June 1937 at Yankton College, Yankton, South Dakota.

"The undeniable defect in a democracy is that the government can rise no higher than the average intelligence of the people," he said. "Unless intelligent leadership can be developed, it must remain mediocre. This explains our heroic attempts at general education to raise the general level of intelligence.

"We strive always to correct the social evils with new laws and therefore laws are passed by the thousands. The success of a democracy depends not on laws but on living up to the moral obligation.

"Many men of high ideals enter political life and find themselves unsupported by men of intelligence. They are underpaid and forced to cater to the unintelligent in order to retain office. For this reason perhaps, the office itself sometimes is regarded with contempt instead of respect. Democracy is safe only so long as culture is in the ascendancy, only so long as the fundamental conception of democracy is recognized as resting on the moral obligation and the conscience of the people rather than on legal enactments.

"At present we throw together in Congress a group of men each educated along his own narrow line. None has a broad general knowledge of the problems of the country. We have been teaching our youth too much memorizing of the things of the past. It does not matter how much knowledge of the principles of medicine, law, engineering, or any other profession a youth may have poured into his memory if he does not know how to use it."

In January 1929 Dr. Will was in Cuba to receive an honorary degree from the University of Havana. After the ceremony, he and Mrs. Mayo went to Santiago, a twenty-six-hour train ride from Havana. While in Santiago, Dr. Will received a cable from Miami, Florida:

TEX RICKARD, SPORTS PROMOTER, CRITICALLY ILL HERE. WILL YOU COME TO ATTEND HIM? PLANE WILL MEET YOU AT HAVANA TO BRING YOU TO MIAMI.

The doctor inquired at once about train schedules. He learned no train would leave for Havana until next day. "There is no use in making the trip if I must wait that long," Dr. Will told his wife. "Rickard is too sick to permit such a delay."

"Then there is nothing you can do," Mrs. Mayo said.

"Nothing, unless I take a plane from here and fly directly to Miami."

"But Will, you've never traveled by plane. I don't want you to do that. I'm afraid it's too dangerous."

Soon another message came to Dr. Will. It appealed to him, again to hurry to Rickard's aid, as the sports promoter was sinking. A plane was being made available at Santiago for him.

"Now that you call me as a surgeon, I will leave in spite of my wife's opinion and will go in the name of humanity," he replied.

Early next morning an airplane left the airport at Santiago carrying the Rochester surgeon at high speed to Miami. The trip was in vain, however, for Rickard died three hours before Dr. Will reached him. The trip was Dr. Will's only airplane flight.

In the same year, 1929, Dr. Charlie performed his last operation. Before donning his surgical uniform on that bright

October morning, he met his son Charles in the corridor leading to the operating amphitheater. "Well son," he said, "today you're taking up where I'm leaving off. This will be my last operation. You are doing your first as a Clinic surgeon. I'm proud to have such a worthy successor. The Mayo name and reputation are in safe hands. Bless you, boy."

Father's and son's hands met in a long, firm clasp.

Dr. Charles Mayo is the third generation of Rochester surgeons. The eldest son of Dr. Charlie, he assisted his father and uncle for four years. He attended Princeton University and the University of Pennsylvania, where he obtained his M.D. degree in 1926. He entered the Mayo Clinic as a Fellow in surgery on July 1, 1927. He also has a son named Charles.

When he was seventy-one years old, Dr. Charlie retired from practice. He believed, with his brother, that the mind failed to keep up with the enthusiasm and visions of youth. Yet there was a certain reluctance to step out. Not long before, he sat in his office eying with full agreement a motto that hung before him. It was a gift from the late Thomas Lipton and read:

THERE IS NO FUN LIKE WORK

"I've always liked that motto, for I believe in it," he said. "To be without work is almost to be without life. For it is work which creates our interest in life. I should be most unhappy to drop contact with the medical profession and the constant changes and discoveries in medicine. For me, the practice of medicine has opened the door to the greatest adventure in life."

Although he knew he was through as a doctor, he never lost his optimism. "The world is making rapid progress along a broad front, as much progress as it is mentally capable of keeping up with," he said. "If we go forward too fast, there is danger that we will lose our way, that we will not be able to value properly each forward step. The world is improving steadily and it's a fair world, a good deal better than no world at all.

"In medicine we have progressed down to the point where, after symptoms have been obtained from a patient, we can study the blood and body secretions in the laboratory and it leads us toward the open door of diagnosis."

Deny as they might that they were geniuses, the world refused to look upon them as anything else. As one commentator said, "The Mayo brothers' genius was unique in that it combined outstanding professional ability with a vision and capacity for organization that had heretofore been effected only in industry—by the Fords, the Rockefellers, the Marshall Fields of the world."

CHAPTER NINETEEN

Sons Honor Father and Mother

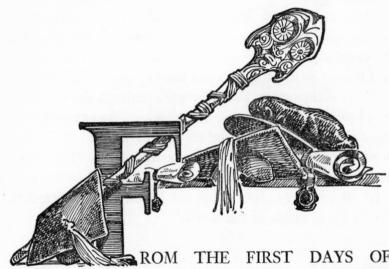

ROM THE FIRST DAYS OF
their success, the Mayo brothers gave credit to their parents
for their achievements. Their father had been a man of high
professional ideals. He instilled in his sons the need of making medicine serve all mankind. He never talked about the
past. His thoughts were always of the future.

The inspiration provided by the physical presence of the
parents lasted far beyond the years of the average family.
Dr. Will and Dr. Charlie were in middle life, had long been
acclaimed for their surgical wizardry, when their father and
mother died. They had the living example of kindly and
gifted parents to stimulate them to philanthropic endeavors.

Touched as they were to do unselfish deeds for others, it
was natural that the brothers should be sentimental. After

their retirement, they decided to reclaim their parental home at Le Sueur, the one built by their father, and preserve it as a public monument.

The house had passed into the hands of C. N. Cosgrove and later was purchased by R. C. Christian. The Mayo brothers bought the dwelling from Mr. Christian and gave it to Le Sueur as a public library. In celebration, the citizens of Le Sueur met in the new high-school auditorium on November 23, 1932. At the same time, a marker was erected outside the Mayo home.

The brothers, together with Dr. Charles, Junior, were guests of the city for the occasion. Willoughby Babcock, curator of the Minnesota Historical Society, Charles M. Babcock, state highway commissioner, and Representative Albert Pfaender of New Ulm, delivered addresses.

Willoughby Babcock paid tribute to the Mayos "not merely for their skill as surgeons and their leadership in the medical profession, but as public-spirited and patriotic citizens. They have always been ready, in times of war and times of peace, to give unstintingly of their time and their resources to every worthy cause."

Charles M. Babcock emphasized the interest the brothers took in the good-roads program. They stressed its importance to medicine because it promoted public health by making accessible hospital care to everyone. For thirty years the Mayos were consistent supporters of every sound and practical good-roads movement, Mr. Babcock pointed out.

The doctors, as always, blushed to hear themselves lauded. Of their own achievements they rarely spoke. But they were always ready to discuss medicine or to talk about others. Dr. Charlie preferred to banter or joke to overcome his embarrassment.

"When they met my train at Rochester this morning as I returned from the East and they told me I would have to give a talk, I said I wasn't born in Le Sueur. But to tell the truth, I wouldn't mind it if I had been."

When Dr. Charlie's son was presented, he commented that "regardless of whether he [Dr. William W. Mayo] was a grandfather of mine, I know these honors you have paid him are a deserved tribute." Then in a lighter vein he added, "While you have placed a marker at the house where my uncle, Dr. Will, was born, I can vouch there are marks all over the house where I was born."

Outside the quaint dwelling, with its gabled windows, stands the marker with a sketch of Dr. Mayo's career in Le Sueur. It reads:

MAYO HOME

In this residence from about 1858 to 1863 lived Dr. William W. Mayo, noted physician and father of the world-famous surgeons, Dr. William J. and Dr. Charles Mayo, the former born here in 1861. During the Sioux attacks on New Ulm in August, 1862, Dr. William W. Mayo acted as surgeon for the defenders.

The sons also honored their father by placing a beautiful stained-glass window in the Eccles Parish church of Manchester, England, in memory of "The Doctor." Dr. Mayo was born in Eccles in 1819. The window was dedicated by Dr. F. Guy Warman, Bishop of Manchester, in a pompous ceremony attended by delegates of the British Medical Association.

When Dr. Charlie was in England for this service, he received the degree of Doctor of Laws from the University of Manchester. He wore a cap and gown of vivid red, with cream-colored trimmings. It became his favorite ceremonial robe and he donned it on numerous occasions when honored later by other educational institutions.

Dr. Will, asked about his most prized ceremonial dress, pointed to a grass skirt given him by the Maoris, aborigines of New Zealand. "See that huge war club?" he asked. "They told me that was my wand of office as 'The Chief.' "

The brothers' endowment of a million and a half dollars for the Mayo Foundation was the outgrowth of "certain definite social obligations" which the elder Mayo had acknowledged and inculcated in his sons. They planned to enlarge this endowment as soon as they were able. In 1935 they contributed another half million dollars to the fund. With accumulated earnings, the endowment totaled two million, eight hundred thousand dollars, "the contribution of the sick of this generation to prevent sickness and suffering in the next," as Dr. Charlie put it.

The brothers continued to travel in their late years and adopted the automobile trailer as their favorite touring vehicle. Dr. Charlie was convinced the trailer was "the best means of escaping taxes yet devised." He said he could hold down expenses by using his "covered wagon," as he termed it.

Yet the brothers owned luxurious trailers and had chauffeurs and cooks in their entourage. In 1936, Dr. Charlie toured eastern United States and Canada and the next year drove to Yankton, South Dakota, to receive a degree from Yankton College.

Despite their frequent trips from home, the Mayos were always anxious to return. "I don't think I could ever live away from Rochester," Dr. Charlie said after a trip to the

Minnesota iron range. "When I return from a tour like this, I ask myself why I went away. I'm satisfied here in Rochester."

Many times the Mayos were asked why they never set up their great medical center in some metropolitan area. Obviously, they were small town boys at heart and they were "satisfied" where they were. But friends and associates saw more behind their refusal to go elsewhere.

"It was partly common sense and partly that higher form of common sense known as genius," a Rochester attorney friend said. "But the Mayo boys had something more than common sense. They were trying everlastingly to improve their work. One of the greatest factors in their success was the way they worked together. When you get teamwork like that, your sum of one and one is many times bigger than two."

An associate of the Mayos gave another explanation. "One reason why they stayed is that they knew the value of old-fashioned friendships," he said. "Will and Charlie were men who kept old friends and who wanted to keep them. They married their wives here. This was home. The land where the Clinic stands was bought by the Old Doctor and it never went out of the Mayo hands. Their roots struck deep."

"The Chief" and Dr. Charlie were great surgeons, but there were and are other great ones. They possessed something more than skill. They had a spirit of achievement that permeated their whole organization. That spirit was implanted in others by Dr. Will and encouraged by Dr. Charlie. Its effect on the Clinic staff was explained by a member.

"They stimulated every man to do the finest work of

which he was capable," the member said. "Staff men were told, 'You may spend whatever you wish. Get what you want when you want it. All we ask is the best possible work.' That is the secret of this institution."

The brothers had a stock answer when asked why they built their clinic in Rochester. "Why should we go to a large city when we have in Rochester all the work we can attend to?" they asked.

"The happiest times of my life were when we were country doctors driving around through the beautiful summer days and calling on patients in the country, patients each of whom was also a friend," Dr. Charlie added.

Even when the Mayos no longer practiced, their name remained magic. Oldsters who came to Rochester to be "taken care of by the Mayo boys" always got to see the surgeons if they persisted. Even in his seventies, Dr. Will "made the rounds" four days a week. Saturdays, Sundays, and Mondays were reserved for motor or boat trips.

If the Mayos refused to leave their own bailiwick to seek fame and fortune in the metropolitan world, the world was not too humble to come to Rochester to honor the Mayos. This it did in 1934 when leaders of commerce, industry, education, government, and medicine, headed by President Franklin D. Roosevelt, visited the surgeons in their home town. It was one of the greatest tributes ever paid to men who served humanity.

CHAPTER TWENTY

Brothers Honored by Nation

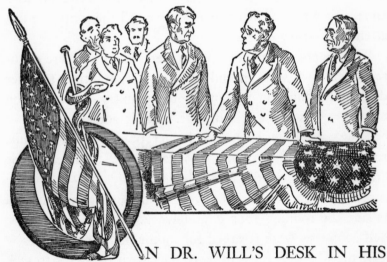

ON DR. WILL'S DESK IN HIS Clinic office stood a small framed motto, the words of the poet Emerson. It was the familiar "mousetrap" aphorism which reads: "If a man can preach a better sermon, write a better book or make a better mousetrap than his neighbor, though he build his house in the woods, the world will make a beaten path to his door."

For fifty years the world had been following a well-marked trail to the Mayo door, first by horse and buggy, then by railroad, later by automobile and airplane. To show their appreciation to the brothers for their great medical feats, universities and colleges the world over had conferred degrees upon them.

At last the day came when the great of the nation would

come to Rochester to pay crowning honors to "the Mayo boys" before the home folk. The National Executive Committee of the American Legion on May 31, 1934, had cited the surgeons "for distinguished service to our sick and disabled comrades and to humanity in general."

To confer that citation upon them, the Legion officials asked President Roosevelt to journey to Rochester, with other notables, to take part in a civic celebration.

August 8 was terrifically hot. Highways leading to Rochester crawled with long lines of motorcars. National Guardsmen and state highway patrolmen sweated in the broiling sun to untangle traffic jams. A hundred thousand persons packed and overflowed the city. They wanted to see the Mayos, the President, the scores of other national dignitaries.

A swarm of visitors surrounded the Chicago and North Western railroad station when the Presidential special arrived. Mr. Roosevelt and his party boarded automobiles and were driven through streets lined with applauding thousands. Scores of maimed and ailing war veterans, in wheelchairs and on crutches, had points of vantage. A few lay on beds suspended from swings over sidewalks. Back of them stood row on row of nurses in freshly starched white. Occasionally one or two dropped from line to assist some spectator overcome by the heat.

The procession moved to the statue of Dr. William Worrall Mayo in Mayo Park, where Mr. Roosevelt placed a wreath at its foot. Next at the Clinic building, a large bronze plaque memorializing the occasion was unveiled by Mayo Walters, grandson of Dr. Will, and Mildred Mayo, granddaughter of Dr. Charlie.

The major event of the day then took place at Soldiers' Field, Rochester's modern playground dedicated to the memory of the war dead. On this spot, where Dr. Will recalled going swimming in the nude in a boyhood escapade and being arrested for his indiscretion, the throng of visitors gathered for the ceremony.

On the platform with the Mayos and President Roosevelt were important men, men of different political faiths who never before had appeared together on a speakers' stand. Medicine, government, education, commerce, industry, and law had sent their ablest and outstanding members.

Edward A. Hayes of Indianapolis spoke for the American Legion as its national leader. Frank B. Kellogg, a schoolmate of the Mayos, came as the American judge of the World Court. Dr. Walter L. Bierring, president of the American Medical Association, and Dr. William D. Haggard, president of the American College of Surgeons, represented the medical profession.

Although they were firm Democrats, the Mayos would not have their big day marred by political rivalries. Floyd B. Olson, Minnesota's youthful governor, was a Farmer-Laborite. Certain members of the arrangements committee objected to his presence and no invitation was sent to him. When they learned of the omission, the Mayos bluntly told the committee their state's chief executive must have a place on the platform. The honors coming to them were honors for the state of Minnesota as well, they insisted, and their governor, no matter to what party he belonged, must appear. The Mayos had their way.

Standing in the merciless sun, the thousands listened patiently to the preliminary speakers. Their pride increased

as they heard the tributes paid to their "Will and Charlie."
At last it was the Legion chief's turn to talk.

"The American Legion is fortunate in having the Mayo
brothers as members, both because of the leadership they
have contributed and because of the material and physical
aid they have rendered in their work of restoring to pro-
ductivity our comrades broken in mind and body," Commander Hayes said.

"Your monuments in this world, over and beyond the
great and magnificent institutions that bear your names, are
the happiness, the love and joy of living you have brought
into the homes by restoration of health to stricken men and
women, rich and poor, in your work."

As he concluded, an expectant quiet fell upon the great
gathering. The busy man, who had traveled from Washington to speak his tribute to two country boys nearing the
close of their remarkable careers, stepped slowly to the
microphones. With a friendly smile, he waited until the
applause ended and then began in vigorous manner to read
from his manuscript.

"I hope that the people of Rochester will not feel limited
in their pride of possession when the nation which I have
the honor to represent claims the right to call Dr. Will and
Dr. Charles by the good name 'neighbor,'" President
Roosevelt began.

Turning to the surgeons, he continued. "You are beloved
at home and abroad, and a world deeply in your debt gives
you inadequate return in external honors and distinctions.
But your true distinction is in the simple fact that you have
put men's sense of brotherhood and interdependence into a
setting and have given it a new meaning.

"For fifty years you have given tireless, skillful and unselfish service here in this state and city. These fifty years, the span of your medical practice, have covered probably the most remarkable period in the history of science. You have seen practically all of modern medicine and surgery come into being. The rise of research, dating back to the days when you began your practice, has revolutionized the diagnosis, prevention and treatment of disease. . . .

"You have seen the growth of hospitals, the creation of foundations for medical research and a revolution in the teaching of medicine. You have seen isolated clinics come to be a part of great universities, an association resulting in the enrichment of both.

"But despite the progress that you have seen and that you have helped to accomplish, the restless spirit of science prompts you to see new visions of achievement. . . .

"In the future development of the curative art, in the discovery of new means for the prevention of disease, in the creation of methods by which all of the people may be made aware of the knowledge of hygiene and public health developed in the laboratory clinic, your visions offer promise of a greater nation and a happier people.

"You have helped to give to the medical profession a unique place in the community and the nation. By reason of his special opportunities, the physician has the occasion to perform a service in his community far beyond the bounds of his own professional duty. His infinitely complex relationships with the people of the community enable him to lead them in standards of ethical right which may profoundly affect human conduct in general.

"For this reason, the science of medicine comes to concern itself with many things besides the healing of the sick. It has been broadly interpreted as a major factor in the science of human welfare. . . .

"Those of us who are concerned with the problems of government and of economics are under special obligation to modern medicine in two very important respects. In the first place, it has taught us that with patience and application and skill and courage, it is possible for human beings to control and improve conditions under which they live. It has taught us how science may be made the servant of a richer, more complete common life. And it has taught us more than that, because from it we have learned lessons in the ethics of human relationship—how devotion to the public good, unselfish service, never-ending consideration of human needs are in themselves conquering forces.

"Democracy looks to the day when these virtues will be required and expected of those who serve the public officially and unofficially. Modern medicine has set an exalted example. It has shown the way for us all.

"You whom we honor today have rendered the highest form of patriotic service during the battles of the World War, but, even more than that, you deserve the nation's thanks for the national service that you have rendered throughout your lives."

Rochester's biggest day thus came to a sweltering end. But it did not end the stream of honors coming to the surgeons. Two years later, eleven hundred doctors gathered in St. Paul to witness the medical profession eulogize the brothers. Bronze medals were presented to the two by Dr. David Riesman, president of the International Medical Assembly of the Interstate Postgraduate Association. The medals—awarded for medical service—before that had been given by the association to only one scientist: Thomas A. Edison.

Dr. Will's remarks, on accepting the medal, epitomize the relentless search of world renowned laboratories for medical truth. "Advances are going to come in the social life of our people and you can't stop them," he said. "Sometimes we have to say to a patient, 'We can't do anything for you today, but tomorrow is another day.'

"Medicine is marching forward. Tomorrow we may have the answer. Tomorrow we may push open the other door."

Dr. Charlie had his own apt manner of describing the endless hunt for new medical marvels. "If I ever found the pot of gold at the end of the rainbow—and that golden pot is the pot of truth—I would be the most disappointed man in the world," he said.

"Truth is not absolute and mathematical. You don't discover it. You put it together. Find a new fact, add a new fact and you have to interpret your truth. It is something you seek—never find."

CHAPTER TWENTY-ONE

Tragedy and Death

They loved the truth and sought to know

THE SPECTACULAR CAREERS of Dr. Will and Dr. Charlie were waning by 1936. Although they appeared at their offices daily, they were forced to lighten their routine to conserve their energies. To escape the rigors of Minnesota's climate, they spent the winters of their last years in the sunshine at Tucson, Arizona.

While it was increasingly evident that the directing hands of the brothers were loosening their holds, there was mounting hope in the house of Mayo that the family tradition would be maintained through another team of eminent medical brothers. Dr. Charlie's two sons, Dr. Charles W. and Dr. Joseph G., were members of the Clinic staff and rapidly rising in skill and esteem in the profession.

Charles had become a Clinic surgeon on the day his father stepped from the operating room for the last time, back in 1929. Joseph had specialized in medicine, the only Mayo to forsake surgery. Together the two were being groomed as a second generation of Mayo brothers well able to perpetuate their name at the Clinic.

In November 1936 Dr. Joseph left Rochester on a hunting trip. On the ninth he was returning home with his favorite hunting dog. When near Cochrane, Wisconsin, his automobile was hit by a Burlington train and the young doctor was killed outright.

The death of Joseph was a severe shock and a sentimental blow to the uncle as well as to the father. Their hopes of being succeeded by a team of brothers were shattered. Today Dr. Charles alone carries on the family name at the Clinic.

The final years exacted a heavy toll of Dr. Charlie. He suffered several strokes, which caused him to limp and he walked with a cane. When he attended commencement exercises at St. Mary's School of Nursing in May 1938, he was under an obvious strain. He appeared to have lost stature and his normal, jolly expression had been somewhat dulled. His dark, appealing eyes lighted, however, with their usual curiosity. Age had scarcely touched his abundant black hair.

Despite his infirmities, Dr. Charlie left Rochester in June to attend the fiftieth graduation anniversary of the Chicago Medical College class of 1888. He treasured the memories of that class, and of all his world-wide honors and degrees, he prized most highly his M.D. diploma from his alma mater.

Dr. Will likewise cherished most dearly his M.D. degree from the University of Michigan. Those certificates represented their father's hopes and ambitions for his boys, and as such they held first place in the sons' affections.

After returning home from Chicago, Dr. Charlie accompanied his brother to Duluth for the annual convention of the Minnesota Medical Association. On July 28 he spoke at a cornerstone-laying ceremony at the new Mayo Civic Auditorium, which he and Dr. Will had given to Rochester.

The latter part of 1938 and the first months of 1939 found Dr. Charlie's health more uncertain. In the fall he suffered an attack of influenza and much concern was felt over his condition. He appeared to have overcome its effects, however, and he and Mrs. Mayo left Rochester, with Dr. and Mrs. Will, for Tucson to spend the cold months.

The winter was a difficult one for Dr. Will. His health became increasingly uncertain, due, it was believed, to a form of amebic dysentery. The ailment persisted until it was discovered that Dr. Will had a serious stomach ulcer. His own diagnosis convinced him it required surgical treatment.

The incidents of early spring pointed to dire events to follow. In March, Sister Mary Joseph, who with Dr. Will and Dr. Charlie formed a famous medical trio at Rochester, became ill. For a quarter of a century the skilled sister stood across the operating table in St. Mary's Hospital from Dr. Will. She had become so proficient that he described her as "easily the first of all our splendid assistants." On March 31 she died.

Dr. Charlie returned home ahead of schedule in the spring of 1939, experiencing his best health in several years. His brother came back in April to prepare for his operation.

Dr. Will began to show the blighting effects of his ailment. While still carrying himself erect and impressive, his sharp features were somewhat dulled. His usually brisk manner was absent and lines had formed in his once-smooth face. His closely trimmed hair appeared whiter.

On reaching home he consulted with his brother and others of the Clinic staff. All agreed he suffered from a subacute perforating gastric ulcer, the treatment of which had been his specialty. An operation was imperative. Dr. Waltman Walters, husband of Dr. Will's daughter Phoebe, was selected for the surgery.

Three weeks after the operation on April 22, the patient left St. Mary's Hospital and a "complete recovery" was predicted. Soon he made brief visits to his office and went on short motor drives, seemingly refreshed physically.

Dr. Charlie, meantime, felt well enough to make a short trip through the Midwest. He arrived in Chicago on May 18 annoyed by a cold. Going to a hotel, he went to bed immediately. The cold suddenly became worse. His family was summoned and, with Dr. Charles, Junior, hurried down from Rochester.

Five prominent Chicago physicians were called in as consultants. They quickly agreed with Dr. Charlie that he had a "bad case of pneumonia." The patient asked to be sent home, by plane if necessary, but he was overruled. It was essential that he be given hospital care immediately.

Breathing with difficulty, Dr. Charlie was wheeled into Mercy Hospital and placed under an oxygen tent. When news was published that the junior partner of America's most famous medical team was fighting for his life, laymen as well as doctors the world over watched the struggle with anxious hearts.

Despite a blood transfusion given by Dr. Charlie's son, the patient failed to rally. It was a hopeless case. For three days the patient was periodically unconscious. The family, grave but reconciled, was gathered at the bedside when death came to Dr. Charlie at 4:55 in the afternoon of Friday,

May 26, 1939, eight days after he was stricken. He had lived two months less than seventy-four years.

Dr. Charles, Junior, announced to waiting reporters that his father had died. "He had no fear of death. He diagnosed his case from the beginning and I think he knew the end was near. He often said his life had been full. He had made people happy and he himself was happy. I know he did not regret going, for he had realized his ambition to relieve all the physical suffering possible during his life."

Charles was asked whether his father had suggested his own treatment. "No, any doctor would be foolish to do that. My father was smart enough to let others treat him as they saw best."

Rochester, staggered by the death of one of its famous "home boys," prepared its final tribute. When the body of Dr. Charlie reached the city on Sunday, it was placed in the Mayo Clinic building, where it lay in state on almost the identical place of his birth. Thousands from Rochester and cities near and far passed the bier.

Mayor Paul A. Grassle proclaimed Monday, the day of the funeral, as a period of sorrow and asked the citizens of Rochester to join in mourning the passing of the noted surgeon. He requested that all business be suspended from three to five o'clock.

Meantime, messages of condolence came to the family from every country and from all classes. Especially numerous were dispatches from Scotland, England, Ireland, and India. Protestant clergymen, Catholic and Episcopal bishops, sent expressions of sympathy.

"I have learned with deep regret of the loss which has come to you [Mrs. Mayo] with such crushing force in the passing of your devoted husband," President Roosevelt said.

"Great surgeon and great humanitarian, Dr. Mayo administered his matchless gifts as a sacred trust for the benefit of all mankind. To you and all who mourn with you, I offer an assurance of sincere sympathy."

The big bronze doors of the Clinic, opened in 1929, were closed for the first time during the hours of the funeral on May 29. Services in Calvary Episcopal Church were followed by burial in Oakwood Cemetery beside the grave of the "Old Doctor."

Dr. Charlie's death was a severe shock to Dr. Will. He was deeply depressed and too ill to attend the funeral services. Life no longer was the same; no longer did it hold the joy of working with a perfect teammate. However, in a few weeks he was about again, making brief visits to his office and riding into the country.

But Dr. Will was seventy-eight and the flame was low. During July he began to "decline and slowly lose his strength." The will to live was ebbing.

On the evening of July 27 the family joined Hattie Mayo at the modest dwelling that had been Dr. Will's home since his more pretentious abode had become the Foundation House. At four o'clock on Friday morning, July 28, Dr. Will died in his sleep. The separation of the "surgical twins" had lasted only two months.

Again Rochester went about its business, sorrowful and pained. The emptiness left by the death of Dr. Charlie was deepened by the new blow. Only the more than six hundred messages eulogizing Dr. Will and extending sympathy lifted the community's lagging spirits.

"Please accept with an assurance of personal sorrow my sympathy in the death of your distinguished husband," President Roosevelt wired Mrs. Mayo. "Like his lamented brother, whose recent passing is still mourned, Dr. Will Mayo combined great skill with a high sense of the beneficent mission of those who practice in the art of healing, and with his brother he will be held in lasting remembrance as a public benefactor. My heartfelt sympathy goes out to you and to members of your family."

Archbishop John Gregory Murray of St. Paul, Minnesota, wired the Mayo family to "Please accept my profound sympathy in your great bereavement." He was joined in this sentiment by a message from the Rev. Hugh O'Donnell, vice president of Notre Dame University at South Bend, Indiana.

"Once more bowed in sorrow with all Rochester, St. John's parish sends sincere sympathy to you and your children who have lost a loved husband and father and the last of Rochester's greater great, Dr. William J. Mayo," Monsignor Garrett P. Murphy, pastor of Rochester's St. John's Catholic Church, said. "He was a great surgeon before surgery itself became great. . . . He not only had a clear insight to every present opportunity and need of service to the sick, but he was an anticipator of future necessity arising out of that broad service to humanity. . . . His name may make history in medicine and surgery, but his works will certainly live after him."

The Knights of Columbus and Sisters of the Catholic Church were likewise represented in the groups extending their sympathies to the Mayos. Edward J. Dooley, grand knight, Rochester council, Knights of Columbus, said: "We send to you an assurance of the council's sympathy in the great sorrow that has come to you and your family. Like every other organization in Rochester, the Knights of Columbus have been proud of everything which your beloved husband and father has accomplished. . . . A truly great man."

"Sincere sympathy and assurance of prayer for your beloved husband from the Sinsinawa Dominican Sisters, who owe so much to his skill and charity," Mother Samuel of River Forest, Illinois, wired. "May God grant him eternal rest."

Mother Mary Gervase of Dubuque, Iowa, telegraphed: "Please accept for myself and bereaved faculty sincere sympathy of all sisters of Mount Carmel, Dubuque, in loss of so great a man and so eminent a physician. He and his brother, Charles, made the name of Mayo a benediction throughout the world. Sweet peace to his great soul."

The funeral was set for Sunday, July 30. Preparations were generally similar to those made for Dr. Charlie. Again the Clinic doors were closed, the second time since they were opened. Mayor Grassle again called on all business to be suspended between three and five o'clock.

The body lay in state in the Foundation House from nine o'clock in the morning until one in the afternoon. Between one and three o'clock Mayo Clinic staff members passed the bier and at four o'clock the final services took place with Congregational and Episcopal clergymen in charge. Burial was in the family lot at Oakwood Cemetery beside Dr. Charlie and Dr. Mayo.

In the center of his working table at the Clinic, Dr. Will had a little framed motto which read:

HE LOVED THE TRUTH AND SOUGHT
TO KNOW IT

"That is going to be on our tombstone—Charlie's and mine," Dr. Will once said.

They loved the truth and they found it.

CHAPTER TWENTY-TWO

They Built a City

A YOKE OF OXEN, DRAGGING
a crude wagon, threshed through the undergrowth along
the Zumbro River in southern Minnesota. Deep-rutted
wagon trails radiated from this crossroads camp ground,
where immigrant trains daily met and parted. A tall, determined man, whip in hand, stalked behind his animals,
urging them to greater speed.

The man was George Head, a homesteader from the
East. He was hard at work that spring day in 1854 clearing
brush from the land bordering the river to map a new town
site. At the head of what is now one of the principal business
streets, he built a log house, the first in the community.
He called his town Rochester, after his home in New York
state.

For two years the wagon trains stopped briefly and then pushed on to more adventuresome regions. Less than fifty persons lived in that pioneer settlement by 1856. But soon many campers who tarried to spend a night or a week in the lush meadows near by lengthened their stay to a month, and then a dozen. In a single year, 1856 to 1857, the population increased to six hundred. The full tide of immigration set in by 1858, when Rochester counted fifteen hundred permanent residents and incorporated itself as a city.

Five years later the country doctor from Le Sueur, Dr. William Worrall Mayo, arrived with his family. Their appearance on the scene, largely unnoticed at the time, was the deciding factor in Rochester's destiny. The city had to wait nearly thirty years before it felt the impact of the pioneering personalities in its midst. But when their influence asserted itself, the course of the community's business and social life was turned to a new and single channel. Rochester became a city whose major industry was caring for the sick. It became a genuine "Doctors' Town."

While civic enthusiasts claim nearly twenty-eight thousand inhabitants for Rochester, the constant transient population more than doubles the official figures. Bed and board are provided annually for more than two hundred and fifty thousand health seekers and their companions by forty hotels, eighty-four apartment houses, two hundred rooming houses and twenty restaurants. A twenty-acre tourist camp shelters twenty thousand travelers each year.

The Mayo Clinic building, two blocks off Broadway, is surrounded by hotels, hospitals, apartment houses, and business buildings. It is the generator that makes Rochester run. It is a pleasant, busy community where the caduceus is the scepter.

The city is as cosmopolitan as any American metropolis and is as well the most sophisticated of its size in the nation. On its streets walk Latin Americans, Europeans, strange-appearing men in white turbans, men and women speaking in foreign tongues. Farmers in overalls, wheat growers from the Red River valley, cowpunchers from Wyoming, celebrities from all nations pass through the Clinic doors. Patients riding in wheelchairs, others with bandaged heads and arms and hands appear on the elm-shaded streets. Shops are modern and offer the latest in style and quality. Motor and bus traffic moves quietly over the paved streets and the honk of a horn is seldom heard.

The rolling loam prairie that surrounds Rochester is surpassed in richness by few Minnesota areas. The heavy soil grows garden products that keep in operation one of the world's largest canneries. Fancy foodstuffs, along with hundreds of gallons of milk, are shipped regularly to eastern markets.

Over this prosperous community watches the Clinic tower, three hundred feet high. From here, at the end of the day, Gregorian chimes and hymns ring out on the twenty-three-bell carillon.

This great humanitarian enterprise, devised by folk-loving doctors, has been made the heritage of a city, a state, and a nation. With their gifts of healing, the Mayos possessed a compelling passion to leave the path smoother for future generations, to reduce suffering, to make people happier. The Mayo Clinic stands symbolic of the success of their endeavors.

Before they died, the Mayo brothers saw the millionth patient pass through the Clinic they and their father established. They often treated famous persons, but in most instances their identity was kept secret.

"The Supreme Court of Condemned Patients" stands as a model of future medical practice. Although the Mayos believed there existed an undesirable trend toward the elimination of the family doctor, the Clinic and similar institutions are moving the profession toward such an end. Health seekers more and more are going to medical centers where specialists in every type of ailment are prepared to study and diagnose their cases.

As one medical authority said, the Clinic has become "a collection of experts, where every department is so arranged that the whole machine can be brought to bear for the benefit of a single case."

On a tree-blanketed elevation south and west of the Clinic building are clustered the homes of the aristocracy of Rochester's streamlined medical workship. Here, on "Pill Hill," live the Clinic bigwigs—the Balfours, the Meyerdings, the Pembertons, the Craigs, the Harringtons, many another medical specialist. To them, and to scores of other associates, the Mayos gave credit for much of their success. They, with Dr. Charles Mayo, carry on the Mayo tradition: "If you do one thing well, though you dwell in the midst of a forest, the world will beat a path to your door."

To Europeans, the Clinic stands as peculiar a contribution to American culture as an automobile factory or a pickle works. To Americans, it stands as a modern medical development in keeping with America's peculiar talent for gaining the most from mass production.

In their fifty-year partnership, the Mayos earned undisclosed millions, but took only a fraction of that wealth for personal use. As philanthropists, they were credited with giving thirteen million dollars toward human welfare and happiness. The three-million-dollar Clinic building represents probably half the value of the Mayo plant, including equipment and laboratories.

When Dr. Charlie's will was filed on June 9, 1939, in Olmsted County Probate Court at Rochester, it listed the value of real and personal property of his estate "in excess of one hundred thousand dollars"—legal terminology indicating possession of considerably larger proportions. Dr. Will's estate, when probated, was similarly left obscure.

Despite the unnumbered Mayo contributions to medical science, some authorities believe the two will be remembered as the founders of a great educational institution after stories of their personal accomplishments are forgotten. They say of Dr. Will, especially, that his fame as an educator and organizer will outlive his renown as a surgeon.

Whatever weight the Mayos may carry with future appraisers, they are thought of today as medical historians—medical geniuses who found surgery in a pioneer stage and made of it a new and skillful art.

Their careers gave new emphasis to the fact that young men seeking important work need not search for it in large cities alone. They demonstrated that lack of opportunity usually meant lack of initiative and energy. Men, not institutions, are the chief need, now as always. Genuine merit finds recognition and with recognition comes appropriate reward.

The Mayos proved, also, that attention to small details contribute largely to success. They promptly adopted the least of minor methods if they produced better work. They willingly obliterated self and lived their lives for others. In this they found the perfect formula for achievement.

On that ideal they founded an institution that stands today as one of the brilliants in an opaque world. A trio of country doctors, possessing a deep love for their fellow men, made a little country town the "Miracle of the Prairies," the "Clinic in the Cornfields" and the "Wonder of the West."

CHAPTER TWENTY-THREE

Honors for the Honorable

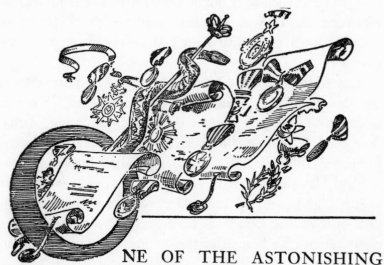

NE OF THE ASTONISHING features of the Mayo careers is the surgeons' extraordinary participation in activities outside their immediate occupations. Honors came to them from seats of learning in all parts of the world. They were feted and decorated as were few others.

They held memberships in medical, military, fraternal, and nonmedical societies and organizations. Dr. Charlie alone was identified with one hundred and sixty groups in various capacities. He was a genial man who loved the company of others, a thirty-second-degree Mason, a member of social clubs in Rochester, Minneapolis, and Chicago. His entry in the 1938 *Who's Who* is the longest in the book.

Dr. Will found less time for outside pursuits, but he nevertheless held nearly fifty memberships, citations, and diplomas. He was one of six founders and charter members of Nu Sigma Nu, medical fraternity, at the University of Michigan. He outlived the other founders. The fraternity was organized during Dr. Will's junior year after medical students became concerned over public misinformation about a classroom prank. It was the first medical-school fraternity founded on a university basis and now has ten thousand members.

The widow of Dr. Charlie, Mrs. Edith Graham Mayo, was designated the "American Mother for 1940." She was honored on Mother's Day by the Golden Rule Foundation "for her leadership qualities directed toward aid for underprivileged children and women everywhere."

Mrs. Mayo is the mother of five children, two foster children, and twelve grandchildren. She was the first president of the Civic League of Rochester and a pioneer in the organization of a branch of the Young Women's Christian Association in Rochester.

When she appeared in New York to accept the honors paid her, she said, "If all the mothers in the world would combine, there wouldn't be any war. They don't know their own strength. Even in countries where women are believed to have a subordinate position, they could prevent war if they would stand firmly against it. As I see it, this is our job— the work is laid out for us."

The activities, degrees, awards, military record, fraternities, memberships, trusteeships, and clubs with which Dr. Charlie was identified follow:

PROFESSIONAL SERVICES

Surgeon and associate chief of staff of Mayo Clinic, Rochester, Minnesota.

Professor of surgery, University of Minnesota Medical School, 1919-1936.

Professor of surgery, University of Minnesota graduate school (The Mayo Foundation), 1915-1936.

Surgeon to St. Mary's, Colonel and Worrall hospitals at Rochester.

UNIVERSITY DEGREES AND FELLOWSHIPS

Northwestern University, M.D. (Doctor of Medicine), 1888.

New York Polyclinic, M.D., 1889.

New York Postgraduate Medical School, certificate, 1890.

American Medical Association, Fellow, 1901.

American Surgical Association, Fellow, 1903.

Northwestern University, M.A. (Master of Arts), 1904.

University of Maryland, LL.D. (Doctor of Laws), *honoris causa*, 1909.

American College of Surgeons, F.A.C.S. (Fellow American College of Surgery), 1913.

Kenyon College, LL.D., *honoris causa*, 1916.

Princeton University, D.Sc. (Doctor of Science), *honoris causa*, 1917.

Royal College of Surgeons of England, F.R.C.S. (Fellow Royal College of Surgeons), 1920.

Northwestern University, LL.D., *honoris causa*, 1921.

Royal College of Surgeons of Ireland, F.R.C.S., 1921.

University of Edinburgh, Scotland, LL.D., *honoris causa*, **1925.**

Queen's University, Ireland, LL.D., *honoris causa*, 1925.

Trinity.College, University of Dublin, Ireland, M.Ch., (master of chirurgery) *honoris causa*, 1925.

University of Pennsylvania, D.Sc., *honoris causa*, 1925.

Royal Society.of Medicine, London, England, F.R.S.M. (Fellow Royal Society of Medicine), 1926.

Detroit College of Medicine and Surgery, D.P.H. (Doctor of Public Health), 1927.

University of Leeds, England, D.Sc., 1929.

University of Manchester, England, LL.D., 1929.

University of Havana, Cuba, M.D., *honoris causa*, 1930.

Hamline University, St. Paul, Minn., LL.D., *honoris causa,*
1930.

University of Notre Dame, South Bend, Indiana, LL.D.,
honoris causa, 1931.

Carleton College, Northfield, Minn., LL.D., *honoris causa,*
1932.

Villanova College, LL.D., *honoris causa,* 1933.

University of South Dakota, LL.D., *honoris causa,* 1934.

University of Minnesota, LL.D., *honoris causa,* 1935.

Yankton College, Yankton, South Dakota, B.S., *honoris causa,*
1937.

REGENT

American College of Surgeons, 1913-1939.

MEDICAL ORGANIZATIONS

American Association for the Advancement of Science.

American Board of Surgery.

American College of Surgeons.

American Genetic Association.

American Medical Association.

American Public Health Association.

American Red Cross.

American Stomatological Association (vice-president 1928-
1930).

American Surgical Association.

Association of Military Surgeons of the United States.

Bronx County Medical Society.

Chicago and North Western Railway Surgeons Association.

Clinical Congress of Surgeons of North America.

Dental Association of New South Wales.

Federation of State Medical Boards of the United States.

Glasgow University Medico-Chirurgical Society.

Gorgas Memorial Institute of Tropical and Preventive Medicine.

International Congress on Tuberculosis (appointed delegate by
governor of Minnesota; president of section on surgery,
1908-09).

International Hospital Association.

Interstate Postgraduate Medical Association of North America (president of clinics, 1924-1939).

La Bienvenue Française, committee on medical schools and hospitals of the American branch.

Minnesota Pathological Society.

Minnesota Public Health Association (board of directors; advisory committee on tuberculosis program).

Minnesota State Medical Association.

New Hampshire Medical Society.

New York and New England Association of Railway Surgeons.

Northwestern University Medical School Alumni Association (president, 1924-1925).

Pan American Medical Association (vice-president, 1931-1935).

Radio Consulting Medical Board of the Second Antarctic Expedition.

Société des Chirurgiens de Paris.

Société Internationale de Chirurgie.

Society of Alumni of Bellevue Hospital, New York.

Society of Clinical Surgery.

Southern Surgical Association.

Western Surgical Association.

Honorary Membership in Medical Organizations

Academia Nacional de Medicina de Buenos Aires.

Accademia Reale Medica di Roma.

American Association for the Study of Goiter.

American Pharmaceutical Association.

Association Internacional Medica, Dental, Farmaceutica de Habla Español.

Association Medica Franco-Mexicana.

Association of Surgeons of Great Britain and Ireland.

El Instituto Médico, Valencia, Spain.

Die Gesellschaft der Ärzte, Wien (Vienna).

Die Gesellschaft der Chirurgen, Wien.

Institute Medica Valenciano.

La Academia Nacional de Medicina de Mexico.

La Comision Provincial Permanente del Hospital de la Facultad de Valencia.
La Société Tchécoslovaquie de Chirurgie et de Gynécologie à Prague.
Manchester Medical Society, Manchester, England.
Medical Library Association.
Minneapolis Surgical Society.
Royal Academy of Medicine, Ireland.
Serbian Medical Society, Belgrade.
Sociedade Brasileira de Urologia.
Sociedad Peruana de Cirujia.

Associate Memberships in Medical Organizations

Académie de Chirurgie de France (formerly the Société Nationale de Chirurgie de Paris).
Minnesota Academy of Science.

Corresponding Memberships in Medical Organizations

Academia Mexicana de Cirugia.
La Real Academia Nacional de Medicina, Madrid, Spain.
La Sociedad Medico-Quirurgical del Guayas.
Sociedad Nacional de Cirujia, Havana, Cuba.
Société des Chirurgiens de Paris.

Presidencies of Medical and Surgical Associations

American College of Surgeons, 1924-1925.
American Medical Association, 1916-1917.
American Surgical Association, 1931-1932.
Chicago and North Western Railway Surgeons Association, 1927-1928.
Clinical Congress of Surgeons of North America, 1914-1915.
Interstate Postgraduate Medical Association of North America, 1934-1935.
Minnesota Public Health Association, 1905-1906.
Society of Clinical Surgery, 1911-1912.
Western Surgical Association, 1904-1905.

SERVICES TO SCIENTIFIC AND NONSCIENTIFIC PERIODICALS

Anales de Cirujia, Havana, Cuba. Foreign collaborator.

Archives of Clinical Cancer Research (member of the educational board, 1924-1939).

Encyclopædia Britannica (member of advisory board, named October 20, 1933).

Gaceta Medica Española (delegate in the United States, 1926-1930; international patron in United States, 1931-1939).

International Clinics (collaborating editor, 1907-1939).

Narkose und Anaesthesie (contributor, 1928-1939).

Nosokomien (member of editorial board).

MILITARY RECORD

Commissioned first lieutenant, M.R.C., United States Army, January 16, 1913.

Commissioned major, medical section, O.R.C., United States Army, April 9, 1917.

Commissioned colonel, medical corps, National Army of the United States, June 15, 1918.

Designated chief consultant, alternating with Colonel William J. Mayo, for all surgical services during the period of participation of the United States in the World War, 1917-1919, medical department of the United States Army, office of the surgeon general.

Received honorable discharge from United States Army on February 28, 1919.

Commissioned brigadier general, Medical Officers' Reserve Corp, United States Army, November 22, 1921.

Commissioned brigadier general, Auxiliary Army of the United States, November 4, 1931.

Assigned on February 18, 1922, as consultant in surgery in the office of the surgeon general in case of emergency. Placed in the branch assignment group, to be called to active duty only under War Department order.

Memberships in Military Organizations

American Legion, William T. McCoy Post No. 92, Department of Minnesota.

Military Order of the World War.

Reserve Officers Association of the United States, Minnesota Chapter.

Veterans of Foreign Wars. Honorary captain of the Whitlock-Sonnenberg Post No. 1215, of Rochester. Veterans of the World War.

Awards

Distinguished Service Medal, United States Army, June 7, 1920.

Officier de l'Ordre National de la Légion d'Honneur (France), 1925.

Officier de l'Instruction Publique et des Beaux-Arts (France), 1925.

Gold Medal of the American Medical Association, 1930.

Cross of Knight Commander of the Royal Order of the Crown of Italy, 1932.

Letter of Commendation, Minnesota State Medical Association, 1934.

Citation in recognition of worthy achievement by Northwestern University Alumni Association, 1934.

Citation for distinguished service by National American Legion, presented by national commander; commemorative plaque presented by President Roosevelt in person, 1934.

Bronze medal for medical service by International Medical Assembly of the Interstate Postgraduate Association, 1936.

Civic and Other Civilian Governmental Offices

Member Minnesota State Board of Health and Vital Statistics, 1900-1902.

Health officer of City of Rochester, 1912-1939.

Member of Rochester School Board, 1915-1923.

MEMBERSHIPS IN NONMEDICAL ORGANIZATIONS

American Asiatic Association.

American Bible Society.

American Geographical Society (Fellow).

American Museum of Natural History (Associate).

American Nature Association.

American Scandinavian Foundation (Associate).

Boy Scouts of America (national councilman and member of committee on health and safety).

Kiwanis Club of Rochester (honorary).

Minneapolis Society of Fine Arts.

Minnesota Congress of Parents and Teachers, Inc.

Minnesota Historical Society (contributing life member).

Minnesota Public Safety Association (made honorary president for life in 1936).

Minnesota State Horticultural Society.

Minnesota Territorial Pioneers (life member).

National Committee of Laymen on Research in Secondary Education.

National Geographic Society.

National Institute of Social Sciences.

National Italian-American Civic League.

Northwestern University General Alumni Association.

Old Owensian Association, Manchester, England (vice president).

Olmsted County Farm Bureau Association.

Olmsted County Old Settlers' Association (vice-president).

Rochester Civic Music Association (honorary president).

Smithsonian Institution, Washington, D. C.

Texas Archeological and Paleontological Society.

Trinity College Association, Dublin, Ireland (life member).

MASONIC AFFILIATIONS

Rochester Lodge No. 21, Ancient Free and Accepted Masons (thirty-second degree).

Zion Commandery No. 2, Knights Templar.

Home Commandery No. 5, Knights Templar.

Winona Consistory No. 4 (Ancient and Accepted Scottish Rites degree).

Halcyon Chapter No. 8, Royal Arch.

Noble of Osman Temple, A.A.O.N. Mystic Shrine, St. Paul, Minn.

Grand Orator, Grand Lodge of Minnesota A.F. and A.M. in 1925.

Grand Representative of the Grand Lodge of New York State, 1924-1939.

Knight Commander of the Court of Honor of the Thirty-second Degree of the Ancient and Accepted Scottish Rite of Freemasonry for the Southern Jurisdiction of the United States, November 10, 1933.

TRUSTEESHIPS

Carleton College, Northfield, Minn. (elected June 6, 1932).

Northwestern University (elected June 11, 1932).

MEMBERSHIPS IN FRATERNITIES

Alpha Kappa Kappa, Psi Chapter at University of Minnesota (honorary member, 1910).

Alpha Omega Alpha, Northwestern University (honorary member, 1927).

Sigma Xi, Mayo Foundation Chapter, University of Minnesota, 1919.

CLUBS

Minneapolis Club, Minneapolis, Minn.

Minnesota Union, University of Minnesota, Minneapolis (life member).

Northwestern University Club of Chicago (honorary).

University Club of Chicago.

University Club of Rochester, Minn.

Dr. Will's affiliations, degrees and honors follow:

PROFESSIONAL SERVICES

Chief of Staff of Mayo Clinic, Rochester.

Surgeon to St. Mary's Hospital, Rochester.

UNIVERSITY DEGREES AND FELLOWSHIPS

American College of Surgeons, Fellow.
Columbia University, D.Sc.
Harvard University, D.Sc.
McGill University, Toronto, Canada, LL.D.
Royal College of Medicine of England, Fellow.
Royal College of Surgeons of England, F.R.C.S.
Royal College of Surgeons of Edinburgh, Scotland, F.R.C.S.
Royal College of Surgeons of Ireland, F.R.C.S.
Trinity College, University of Dublin, Ireland, doctor of science
   in chirurgery.
University of Leeds, England, D.Sc.
University of Maryland, LL.D.
University of Michigan, M.A.
University of Michigan, M.D.
University of Michigan, D.Sc.
University of Minnesota, LL.D.
University of Notre Dame, LL.D.
University of Pennsylvania, LL.D.
University of Pittsburgh, LL.D.
University of South Dakota, LL.D.
University of Toronto, LL.D.
Villanova College, LL.D.

REGENT

University of Minnesota, 1907-1939.

MEMBERSHIPS AND OFFICES IN MEDICAL ORGANIZATIONS

American Association for the Advancement of Science.
American College of Surgeons (president, 1917-1919).
American Medical Association (president, 1905-1906).
American Surgical Association (president, 1913-1914).
Congress of American Physicians and Surgeons (president,
   1925).
Minnesota State Medical Association (president, 1893-1894).
Society of Clinical Surgery (president, 1911-1912).

HONORARY MEMBERSHIPS IN MEDICAL ORGANIZATIONS

Association of Surgeons of Great Britain and Ireland.
Copenhagen Medical Society, Denmark.
Edinburgh Medico-Chirurgical Society, Scotland.
La Academia Nacional de Medicina, Mexico.
Sociedad Peruana de Cirurgia.
Serbian Medical Society, Belgrade.

ASSOCIATE MEMBERSHIPS IN MEDICAL ORGANIZATIONS

Royal Academy of Medicine of Rome (academician).
Société Nationale de Chirurgie de Paris (associate foreign member).

CORRESPONDING MEMBERSHIPS IN MEDICAL ORGANIZATIONS

Academia Nacional de Medicina de Buenos Aires.
La Societa Medico-Chirurgica di Bologna, Italy.
Sociedad de Cirujia de Buenos Aires.

MILITARY RECORD

Colonel and chief consultant for all surgical services during the World War, 1917-1919, in the medical department of the United States Army.
Brigadier general in the Medical Officers' Reserve Corps, United States Army, 1921.

AWARDS

Distinguished Service Medal, United States Army, 1920.
Commander of the Royal Order of the North Star (honor instituted by King Frederik of Sweden in 1748).
Gold Medal of the National Institute of Social Sciences.
Bronze Medal for medical service from International Medical Assembly of the Interstate Postgraduate Association.
Henry Jacob Bigelow gold medal of the Boston Surgical Society.

FRATERNITIES

Phi Beta Kappa.
Sigma Xi.

Bibliography

BOOKS

CLAPESATTLE, HELEN. *The Doctors Mayo.* Minneapolis: University of Minnesota Press, 1941.

Committee Upon the Relation of the Medical School with the Mayo Foundation, The Medical School of the University of Minnesota and the Mayo Foundation for the Promotion of Medical Education and Research.

Division of Publications, Mayo Clinic, Rochester, Minn. *Sketch of the History of the Mayo Clinic and the Mayo Foundation.* Philadelphia and London: W. B. Saunders Company, 1926.

FOLWELL, WILLIAM WATTS. *History of Minnesota.* St. Paul, Minn.: Minnesota Historical Society, 1922. Vol. 2.

HARPER, HENRY HOWARD. *Merely the Patient.* New York: Minton, Balch & Co., 1930.

————. *Lectures (on the history of medicine).* Philadelphia and London: W. B. Saunders Company, 1926-1932.

MARTIN, DR. FRANKLIN H. *The Joy of Living.* Garden City, N. Y.: Doubleday, Doran & Co., Inc., 1933. Vol. 2.

MAYO, CHARLES H. AND WILLIAM J. *A Collection of Papers Published Previous to 1909.* Philadelphia and London: W. B. Saunders Company, 1912. Two volumes.

MAYO, CHARLES H. AND HENRY W. PLUMMER. *The Thyroid Gland.* St. Louis: The C. V. Mosby Company, 1925.

MAYO, WILLIAM J. *Contributions of the Nineteenth Century to a Living Pathology, Ether Day Address.* Boston: The Batra Press, 1912.

MAYO CLINIC MONOGRAPHS. Philadelphia and London: W. B. Saunders Company.

MELLISH-WILSON, MRS. MAUD H., RICHARD M. HEWITT and LLOYD G. POTTER. *Collected Papers of the Mayo Clinic, 1905-1932.* Philadelphia and London: W. B. Saunders Company. (Published under various titles: 1905/09-1913—*Collected Papers by the Staff of St. Mary's Hospital, Mayo Clinic, Rochester, Minn.* 1914-1922—*Collected Papers of the Mayo Clinic, Rochester, Minn.* 1923—*Collected Papers of the Mayo Clinic and the Mayo Foundation.*)

———. *Minnesota, American Guide Series.* New York, Viking Press, 1938.

———. *Physicians of the Mayo Clinic and the Mayo Foundation.* St. Paul and Minneapolis, Minn.: The Bruce Publishing Company, 1923.

———. *Physicians of the Mayo Clinic and the Mayo Foundation.* Philadelphia and London: W. B. Saunders Company, 1927-37.

———. *Physicians of the Mayo Clinic and the Mayo Foundation.* Minneapolis: The University of Minnesota Press, 1937; London: Oxford University Press.

———. *Proceedings of the Staff Meetings of the Mayo Clinic,* January, 1927–December, 1940. Rochester, Minn.

RODGER, ESCA G. *Careers.* New York: D. Appleton and Company, 1928.

WILDER, LUCY. *The Mayo Clinic.* Minneapolis: The McGill Lithograph Company, 1936. Revised edition—New York: Harcourt, Brace & Co., 1941.

———. *The Mayo Clinic.* New York: Harcourt, Brace & Co., 1938.

MAGAZINE ARTICLES

"America's Most Noted Surgeons," *Hampton Magazine,* Vol. 24 (May 1910), page 689.

"American Mother of 1940 (Mrs. Charles H. Mayo)," *Newsweek,* Vol. 15 (April 29, 1940), page 4.

"Aviation Medicine Laboratory Opened at Mayo Clinic," *Science News Letter,* Vol. 35 (May 6, 1939), page 279.

BENNETT, JAMES O'DONNELL. "Superlative Americans," *Chicago Tribune* Sunday Magazine Section, 1923.

BRECHER, EDWARD M. "Dr. Will and Dr. Charlie," *Scribner's Commentator*, July 1940; condensed in *Reader's Digest*, Vol. 37 (July 1940), page 43.

BREEN, MARGUERITE. "Dr. Charles H. Mayo Made Great Contribution to Minnesota's Fight Against Tuberculosis," *Everybody's Health*, Vol. 24 (June-July 1939), page 2.

CLAPESATTLE, HELEN. "Health and Medicine in Rochester, 1855–70," *Minnesota History*, Vol. 20 (September 1939), page 221.

CUSHING, H. "Mayo Brothers and Their Clinic," *Science*, Vol. 90 (September 8, 1939), page 225.

"Doctor Charlie," *Time*, Vol. 33 (June 5, 1939), page 78.

"Dr. Mayo Home of Early Days Draws Throng," *St. Paul Dispatch*, Nov. 23, 1932.

"Dr. W. J. Mayo and the Board of Regents of the University of Minnesota," *School and Society*, Vol. 45 (March 6, 1937), page 322.

DOUGLAS, ROBERT. "A Clinic on Minnesota's Prairies," *The New York Times Magazine*, October 21, 1928.

FITZGERALD, J. V. "The Boyhood of Famous Americans," *The Minneapolis Tribune*, August 2, 1930.

GRENFELL, DR. WILFRED T. "Two Leaders in Surgery," *Outlook*, Vol. 86 (June 22, 1907), page 404.

HAUN, JULIUS W. "Mercy Rides the Clouds: Founding of St. Mary's Hospital and the Mayo Clinic," *Commonweal*, Vol. 25 (February 12, 1937), page 435.

"Insanity the Price of Civilization, C. H. Mayo Says," *The St. Paul Dispatch*, October 15, 1931.

"Is There A Soul? Yes, Says Dr. Mayo," *The St. Paul News*, December 31, 1926.

"Lectures Before the Mayo Foundation," *Science*, Vol. 70 (November 15, 1929), page 473.

LEFKOVITZ, HERBERT. "Elder Statesmen of American Medicine," *The New York Times Magazine* (July 19, 1936).

"Legion Honors Doctors Mayo with Citation," *The St. Paul Dispatch* (August 8, 1934).

"Mayo Brothers Give Millions in Cash," *Men of Minneapolis* (September 11, 1930).

"Mayo Brothers, Masters of Efficiency," *Independent*, Vol. 88 (October 16, 1916), page 92.

"Mayo Clinic and Foundation Organized to Carry on Work," *Science News Letter*, Vol. 36 (August 12, 1939), page 109.

"Mayo Clinic Birthplace to Celebrate Half a Century of Progress in Surgery," *Newsweek*, Vol. 14 (October 23, 1939), page 38.

"Mayo Clinic Publicity," *Time*, Vol. 30 (August 16, 1937), page 32.

"Mayo Foundation Hit by State Physicians as Disturbing Force," *The Minneapolis Tribune* (March 24, 1917).

MAYO, CHARLES H. "Before and After Forty," *Rotarian*, Vol. 50 (June 1937), page 24.

———. "Doctor and His Patients," *Hygeia*, Vol. 7 (April 1929), page 347.

———. "French Achievement in Surgery and Medicine, *World's Work*, Vol. 34 (October 1917), page 602.

———. "How to Live Longer," *Hygeia*, Vol. 9 (October 1931), page 907.

———. "It's the Brain That Counts," *Journal of the National Education Association*, Vol. 19 (November 1930), page 258.

———. "Surgery and Orthopedics," *Charities and the Commons*, Vol. 21 (November 7, 1908), page 191.

"Mayos' Contribution to Medical Research and Practice," *Scientific Monthly*, Vol. 49 (October 1939), page 378.

MAYO, WILLIAM J. "Do You Fear Cancer?" *Delineator*, Vol. 98 (April 29, 1921), page 35.

———. "Aims and Ideals of the American Medical Association," *Journal of the National Education Association for 1928*, page 158.

———. "Education and Opportunity," *Vital Speeches*, Vol. 2 (July 1, 1936), page 616.

———. "Function of Medical Schools Is to Turn Out General Practitioners," *School Life*, Vol. 13 (November 1927), page 41.

Bibliography 237

MAYO, WILLIAM J. "How Our Senses Help Us," *Hygeia*, Vol. 8 (November 1930), page 1033.

———. "Medical Conditions in South America," *Bulletin of the Pan American Union*, Vol. 52 (January 1921), page 48.

———. "Right to Health," *North American*, Vol. 211 (February 1920), page 194.

———. "Senses in Science," *Hygeia*, Vol. 5 (July-August 1927), page 343.

———. "The Medical Profession and the Issues Which Confront It," *Science*, Vol. 23 (June 16, 1906), page 897.

MELONEY, MRS. W. B. "Mrs. Mayo, Wilderness Mother," *Delineator*, Vol. 85 (September 1914), page 9.

MULLETT, MARY B. "Dr. Will and Dr. Charlie," *American Magazine*, Vol. 85 (February 1918), page 10.

"Obituary of Charles H. Mayo," *Newsweek*, Vol. 13 (June 5, 1939), page 40.

"Obituary of William J. Mayo," *Newsweek*, Vol. 14 (August 7, 1939), page 37.

"Obituary of William J. Mayo, "*School and Society*, Vol. 50 (August 12, 1939), page 205.

"Obituary of William J. Mayo," *Time*, Vol. 34 (August 7, 1939), page 38.

"Obligations of Wealth," *Belleman*, Vol. 23 (September 22, 1917), page 313.

PARSONS, E. DUDLEY. "Leaders of Minnesota Progress," *The Minneapolis Journal*, February 29, 1920.

PETERSON, E. T. "Dr. Mayo Tells How to Live," *Better Homes and Gardens*, Vol. 12 (April 1934), page 16.

Portraits of Charles H. Mayo:

Collier's, Vol. 84 (December 14, 1929), page 10.
Current Opinion, Vol. 78 (January 1925), page 6.
Harper's Weekly, Vol. 57 (July 4, 1913), page 9.
Literary Digest, Vol. 123 (April 10, 1937), page 18.
Munsey, Vol. 48 (February 1913), page 741.
Newsweek, Vol. 14 (October 23, 1939), page 39.
Review of Reviews, Vol. 58 (July, 1918), page 15.

Rotarian, Vol. 50 (January 1937), page 39.

World's Work, Vol. 32 (September 1916), page 479.

Portraits of William J. Mayo:
   Better Homes and Gardens, Vol. 12 (April 1934), page 17.
   Literary Digest, Vol. 103 (November 9, 1929), page 28; Vol. 123 (April 10, 1937), page 19.

Portraits of William Worrall Mayo:
   American Magazine, Vol. 85 (February 1918), page 12.
   Scientific Monthly, Vol. 49 (October 1939), page 378.

"Rochester, a City of Wheelchairs," *The Minneapolis Journal*, (August 28, 1921).

"Skill As Surgeon Brought Dr. Mayo Worldwide Fame," *Rochester Post-Bulletin* (July 28, 1939).

SMITH, FRANK. "Frank Smith's Story of the Mayo Clinic," *Chicago Daily Times*, Vol. 8, No. 268 (July 19, 1937–August 8, 1937).

Staff Bulletin of the Mayo Clinic, March, 1934.

STEWARD, THOMAS E. "Dr. Mayo an Outstanding American of His Time," *The Minneapolis Tribune* (July 29, 1939).

TAFT, W. H. "Work of the Mayo Brothers," *Science*, Vol. 51 (June 4, 1920), page 569.

"The Facts From Both Sides on the Medical School Controversy," *The Minnesota Alumni Weekly*, Vol. 20 (January 6, 1921), page 13.

"The Mayo Foundation and the University of Minnesota," *The Outlook*, Vol. 110 (June 23, 1915), page 400.

"The Medical School in British Eyes," *The Minnesota Alumni Weekly*, April 28, 1921.

"The University's Mayo Foundation Research Center," *Minnesota Chats* (June 1928).

"Tribute Paid Dr. Will as Friend of Education and Great Executive," *The Minneapolis Tribune*, July 29, 1939.

"Two Brothers Who Have Performed a Wonder of the Medical World," *Current Opinion*, Vol. 64 (March 1918), page 177.

"University of Minnesota and the Mayo Foundation," *School and Society*, Vol. 2 (July 3, 1915), page 26.

"University of Minnesota and the Mayo Foundation," *Science*, Vol. 41 (June 11, 1915), page 855.

WALSH, JAMES J. "A Medical Pilgrimage Westward," *The Independent*, Vol. 71 (July 27, 1911), page 189.

WILSON, L. B. "William Worrall Mayo: A Pioneer Surgeon of the Northwest," *Surgery, Gynecology and Obstetrics* (May 1927).

NEWSPAPER ARTICLES

The Boston Transcript: June 4, 1921.

The Chicago Tribune: September 14, 1917.

The Christian Science Monitor: March 21, 1934; April 18, 1940.

The Minneapolis Journal: July 7, 1916; March 26, 1917; October 1, 1933; February 18, 1934; May 27, 1939; July 28, 1939.

The Minneapolis Star: March 19, 1924; May 21, 1936; July 20, 1936; May 27, 1939; July 28, 1939.

The Minneapolis Tribune: March 28, 1917; April 15, 1917; November 12, 1924; April 27, 1930; May 27, 1939.

The New York Times: September 14, 1917; May 22, 1936; June 8 and 9, 1936; July 19, 1936; April 23, 1939; May 20, 1939; May 26, 27, 28, 29, 30, 1939; June 10, 1939; July 29, 31, 1939; October 12, 14, 1939.

The New York Tribune: June 14, 1923.

The St. Paul Dispatch: October 15, 1930; July 18, 1937; May 27, 1939; July 28, 1939.

The St. Paul News: July 2, 1937.

The St. Paul Pioneer-Press: October 21, 1924; June 18, 1935; May 27, 1939.

BIOGRAPHICAL SKETCHES OF THE MAYOS

American Magazine (C. H. & W. J. Mayo), Vol. 115 (May 1933), page 39.

American Medical Biographies (W. W. Mayo), Baltimore: The Norma, Remington Company, 1920.

The Columbia Encyclopedia (C. H. & W. J. Mayo), New York: Columbia University Press, 1935.

The Cyclopedia of American Biography (C. H. & W. J. Mayo),

Supplementary Edition, New York: The Press Association Compilers, Inc., 1928. Vol. 11.

Dictionary of American Biography (W. W. Mayo), New York: Charles Scribner's Sons, 1933. Vol. 12.

The Encyclopedia Americana (C. H. & W. J. Mayo), New York and Chicago: Americana Corporation, 1932.

The Encyclopædia Britannica (C. H. & W. J. Mayo), Fourteenth Edition. London and New York: The Encyclopædia Britannica Company Ltd., 1929.

Encyclopedia of American Biography (C. H., W. J., & W. W. Mayo), New Series. New York: The American Historical Company, Inc., 1940.

Minnesota and Its People (C. H., W. J., & W. W. Mayo), Chicago: The S. J. Clarke Publishing Company, 1924. Vol. 3.

Minnesota, Its Story and Biography (C. H., W. J., & W. W. Mayo). Chicago and New York: The Lewis Publishing Company, 1915. Vol. 3.

The National Cyclopædia of American Biography (C. H. & W. J. Mayo). New York: James T. White & Co., 1930. Current Vol. A.

The National Encyclope of American Biography (W. W. Mayo), 1924.

The New International Encyclopædia (C. H. & W. J. Mayo), Second edition. New York: Dodd, Mead and Company, 1926. Vol. 15.

The New International Year Book for 1939 (C. H. & W. J. Mayo). New York and London, Funk & Wagnalls Company, 1940.

New Standard Encyclopedia of Universal Knowledge (C. H. & W. J. Mayo). New York and London: Funk & Wagnalls Company, 1931. Vol. 18.

Who's Who in America (C. H. & W. J. Mayo), 1938-39. Chicago: The A. N. Marquis Company, 1938. Vol. 20.

Who's Who in American Medicine (C. H. & W. J. Mayo). New York: Who's Who Publications, Inc., 1925.

The World Book (C. H. & W. J. Mayo). Chicago and Kansas City: Roach and Fowler, Publishers, 1922. Vol. 6.

Index

A

Accidents, 60, 61, 116, 176, 183, 208
Advertising, 73, 104, 108, 109; ethics of, 103
Alcohol, 168, 174
American College of Surgeons, 106, 185, 202
— Dental Association, 185
— Legion, 201-203; William T. McCoy Post, 148
— life, 183, 185, 188, 218
— Medical Association, 106, 114, 161, 167, 202
— Surgical Association, 161
Amphitheater, operating, 157, 192
Anesthesia, 92
Anesthetic, 68, 69, 90, 96, 125, 158, 159
Anesthetist, 68, 85, 122
Antisepsis, 129
Antiseptic surgery, 53-54, 90
"Apostle of Protest," 57
Appendicitis, 121
Army, United States, 12, 52; scouts, 12; surgeon, 106, 107; brothers in, 144, 145; medical department, 146, 148
Ashburn, General T. Q., 174
Assistants, 86, 113, 138, 158, 159; training of, 112
Associate, 113, 154, 155, 198; surgeon, 113
Automobile, 115, 172, 197, 200, 201, 208, 218
Autopsy, 58
Avocation, 185

B

Babcock, Charles M., 195
Babcock, Willoughby, 195
Baker, Howard, 26; Martha, 26
Balfour, Dr. Donald C., 113, 174, 218
Beckman, Dr. Emil H., 113
"Bedside manner," 166

Bellevue Hospital, New York, 54, 55, 64
"Belly doctor," 112
Benson, Senator Henry N., 140
Berkman, Dr. David M., 139
Bierring, Dr. Walter L., 202
Blake, Dr. Joseph A., 121, 124, 125
Brewer, Dr. G. E., 124
British Medical Association, 196
Brothers, 77, 78, 92, 100, 103, 108, 111, 118, 119, 120, 121, 125, 129, 132, 134, 136, 141, 145, 150, 160, 163, 164, 165, 177, 194, 195, 197, 198, 200, 207; in war, 144, 146; eulogy of, 205
Byford, Dr. William Heath, 21

C

Cancer, 106, 110, 183, 184, 188; causes of, 107, 108; of stomach, 112, 162; treatment of, 188
"Carbolic spray," 53
Cataract, 76, 83, 98, 159
Catholic, 98; clergymen, 211; mission, 85; sisters, 80, 82, 84, 85, 87, 89, 94
Central Public School, 63, 70
Charity, 89, 90, 141, 156, 174; patients, 130
Chicago, Illinois, 22, 74, 82, 83, 84, 95, 99, 106, 110, 111, 122, 123, 124, 164, 175, 209, 210, 221
Chicago Medical College, 83; fiftieth anniversary, 208
Children, 149, 174, 176, 222
Cholecystitis, 121
Cholera Morbus, 73
Christian, R. C., 195
City Council, 80, 133
Civic League, Rochester, 222
Clamp, technique invented, 67
Clark, Ida, 92
Clinic. See Mayo Clinic
"Clinic in the Cornfields," 220
Collins, Homer, 92
Colon, 161
Consultants, 145, 148, 157, 189, 210

Coroner, 57, 58
Country doctors, 187, 199, 216, 220

D

Dalton, John, 20
Damon, Eleazer, 83; Hattie M., 83
Death, 162, 208, 209, 210, 212
Deming, Dr. Eleazar, 20
Dentistry, 185
Diagnosis, 128, 156, 157, 158, 159, 182, 183, 193, 209
Diagnostician, 96, 97
Dissection, 59, 73
"Doctors' Town," 216
Dodd, Captain W. W., 39
Donnelly, Ignatius, 57
Dooley, Edward J., grand knight, Rochester Knights of Columbus, 213
Drake, Colonel J. L., 5, 7, 8, 9, 10, 15; farm, 4
Duct, 161
Duodenum, 161, 162
Dysentery, 73, 209

E

Easterman, Dr. George B., 139
Eaton, Burt, 103
Edgar, John, 71, 72
Edison, Thomas A., 206
Edith. See Mrs. Charles H. Mayo
Education, 63, 69, 70, 73, 83, 84, 96, 102, 142, 149, 150, 179, 190; system, 186
Ellison, Charles, 63
Emerson, Ralph Waldo, 200
Endowment, 102, 135, 136, 137, 186, 197
Epidemics, 142, 150
Episcopalian, 98, 169; clergymen, 211, 214
Esophagus, 109
Ether, 68
European, 217, 218; surgeons, 84

F

Faes, A. A., 123
"Father of Medicine," 180
Fees, 100, 101, 130, 131, 132, 133
Fellowship, 137, 139, 155
Fellows of Mayo Clinic, 138; pay of fellows, 155, 176; Dr. Charles Mayo, Jr., 192
Fenger, Dr. Christian, 84; teaching clinic, 84
Flandrau, Judge Charles E., 29, 30, 31, 33, 34, 35, 37, 38, 39, 44
Foundation, 102, 148, 204
Foundation for Medical Education and Research, Mayo, 103, 138, 150. See also Mayo

Foundation House, 176, 212, 214
Franciscan Sisters, 80, 82, 84, 85, 88, 95, 99
Friendship, 198
"Frontier Guard," 36, 40

G

Galbraith, Joseph, 17, 18
Gall bladder, 110, 121, 158, 161
Galtier, Father Pierre, 22
General surgeon, 113, 155
Germs, 53, 54, 130
Gland treatment, 182
Goiter, 91, 112, 159, 162, 173
Golden Rule Foundation, 222
Gorgas, Surgeon General William Crawford, 145
Gorman, W. A., 23
Graham, Dr. Christopher, 96, 119; Miss Edith, 95
Grassle, Mayor Paul A., 211, 214

H

Haggard, Dr. William D., 202
Hartzell, John, 176
Harwick, Harry J., 130
Hayes, Edward A., 202, 203
"Head doctor," 112
Head, George, 215
Health officer, 133
Henderson, Miss Florence, 122, 123
Hernia, 159, 161
Hill, James J., 10
Hill, Dr. S. R., 181
Hippocrates-Mayo, 160
Hobbies, 171, 174, 175
Holstein, 171
"Holy money," 102, 141
Homeopath, 155
Homes, 77, 78, 79, 80, 90, 91, 115, 127, 171, 200
Honeymoon, 95
Hospital, 73, 78; for tornado victims, 79; intern, 73, 96, 97, 113; new hospital proposed, 81, 84; private, 84; rival, 94. See also St. Mary's Hospital
Humor, 106, 118, 120, 172
Hyacinth, Sister, 85
Hyde, Dr. W. A., 52

I

Incision, 60, 68, 84
Indian, 12, 13, 14, 16, 17, 19, 23, 28, 31, 36, 40; burial, 48; condemned to death, 46; hanged, 47, 48; motto, 47; treachery, 39; trial, 46, 47

Indian massacres, 8, 12, 14, 27; toll of, 46
Indians, Sioux, 11, 12, 13, 16, 19, 25, 26, 27; prisoners of, 45
Infection, 53, 54; focal, 184-185
Influenza, 73
Inland Waterways Corporation, 174
Insanity, 185, 186
Instruments, 91, 158
International Medical Assembly of the Interstate Postgraduate Association, 205
Intestines, 159, 161, 172
Invective, 72

J

Johns Hopkins, 110
Johnson, Governor John A., 138
Jones, Robinson, 25, 26
Judd, Dr. Edward Starr, 113, 139
Judge, 115

K

Kahler Corporation, 134
Kahler, John H., 134
Kellogg, Frank B., 202
Kidney, 73, 162
Koch, Robert, 129

L

La Bathe, Francis, 18
Laboratories, 113, 128, 157, 159, 180, 193, 204, 206; assistants, 150
Laparotomies, 67
Law, Dr. Arthur A., 160
Le Sueur, Minnesota, 3, 4, 8, 9, 10, 11, 13, 15, 29, 31, 33, 40, 45, 50, 216; Mayo home reclaimed, 195-196
Lincoln, President Abraham, 46, 143
Lipton, Thomas, 192
Liquor, 168, 173, 176
Lister, Sir Joseph, 53, 54, 73, 129, 179
Little Crow, Chief, 17, 18, 26, 27, 28, 29, 36, 38, 39, 45
Liver, 158
Livermore, Fred, 88
Lungs, 73

M

McCarthy, Dr. William Carpenter, 159
McDowells Medical College, 21
Maclean, Professor Donald, 73
"Made in Germany," 182
Manchester, England, 191, 196; University of, 20

Mankato, Minnesota, 40, 44, 45, 46, 47, 48
Martin, Dr. Franklin H., 106, 146
Mary Joseph, Sister, 85, 86, 88; illness and death of, 209
Mastoid, 98
"Mayo Boys," 9, 60, 106, 199, 200
Mayo, Carrie, daughter of Dr. Will, 174
— Dr. Charles Horace, 9, 14, 55, 56, 57, 63, 70; birth of, 53; as father's assistant, 58, 64, 67, 68; as studious youth, 62; as youthful inventor, 62; as grade-school pupil, 63; as anesthetist, 68; as partner in Mayo business, 74; in tornado, 76-79; begins medical college training, 83; obtains doctor's degree, 84; postgraduate study, 84; on St. Mary's Hospital medical staff, 85; inventive genius of, 86; as hospital nurse, 88; builds hospital elevator, 88; views on hospital policy, 89; surgical success, 90; first goiter operation, 91; performs five thousand goiter operations, 92; refuses nomination as coroner, 93; marriage of, 95; author of medical papers, 97; his operations and skill, 98; praise of Catholic sisters, 99; seeks use for money, 100; habits of dress, 105; appearance of, 106, 118, 119, 208; as "universal specialist," 112; honors to, 114; gravely ill, 117; chief characteristics, 119; as speaker, 119; as jokester, 120; rights of brothers, 129; placed on salary, 129; becomes Rochester health officer, 133; elected to school board, 134; creates endowment, 137; commission in Army, 144; organizes wartime hospital base, 146; indifference to Army etiquette, 146; awarded Distinguished Service Medal, 147; polishes guests' shoes, 148; honesty with patients, 150, 157; decides on larger Clinic, 151; a surgeon's day, 157-159; known universally as Dr. Charlie, 165; interest in music, 170; secret of keeping fit, 171; Mayowood, 171; address to farmers, 172; large family, 176; sons follow father's career, 176; leader in medicine, 179; boomed for President, 181; medicine as unfinished field, 182; views on gland treatment, 182; retirement of, 182; views on changes in medi-

cine, 183; criticizes overeating, 184; concern over increase in insanity, 185; role of public-health education, 187-188; help to others, 189; views on democracy, 190; performs last operation, 191-192; finds fun in work, 192; retains optimism, 192-193; praised by state officer, 195; honors father, 196; increases foundation endowment, 197; travels by trailer, 197; why the Mayos stayed in Rochester, 198-199; country-doctor days, 199; cited by American Legion, 201; lauded by President Roosevelt, 203-205; son killed, 208; suffers ill health, 208, 209; stricken with pneumonia, 210; death of, 210, 211; earnings of, 218; contribution to medical education, 219; value of estate, 219; termed medical historian, 219; honors and citations of, 222-230
— Mrs. Charles Horace, 96, 121, 125, 209, 222
— Dr. Charles W., Jr., 146, 176, 192, 195, 207, 208, 210, 211, 218
— Charles III, 192
— Civic Auditorium, 116, 148, 170, 209
— Clinic, 8, 9, 52, 63, 90; "Clinic in the Cornfields," 8, 220; the medical lodestone, 8; "The Supreme Court of Condemned Patients," 8, 218; twenty-seven thousand goiter patients, 92; standards, 97; hallways, 120; site selected, 126; first Clinic building, 126; policy of, 127; how Clinic developed, 128; fee system, 130; Fellows of the Mayo Clinic, 138; ideal of, 141; income, 142; possessions put under Mayo Properties Association, 148, 149; larger building needed, 151; new building, 153, 154; how Clinic is governed, 154-155; routine of patients in, 156, 157; search for information, 188; Dr. Charles W. Mayo, Jr., joins, 192, 198; plaque unveiled, 201; body of Dr. Charlie in Clinic, 211; doors closed for funeral, 212, 214; hub of Rochester, 216, 217; symbolic of Mayo success, 217; defined by authority, 218; appraisal of, 218; value of, 218
— Dorothy, daughter of Dr. Charlie, 176
— Edith, daughter of Dr. Charlie, 176
— Esther, daughter of Dr. Charlie, 176

— firm, 84, 96
— Gertrude Emily, daughter of Dr. W. W. Mayo, 11, 21, 33, 41, 50, 61, 62
— Dr. Herbert, 20
— James, father of Dr. W. W. Mayo, 19
— John, adopted son of Dr. Charlie, 176
— Dr. Joseph G., son of Dr. Charlie, 176, 207, 208
— Louise, daughter of Dr. Charlie, 176
— Marilyn, adopted daughter of Dr. Charlie, 176
— Mildred, granddaughter of Dr. Charlie, 201
— office, 79, 94, 99, 112, 114, 136, 200
— Park, 116, 201
— Phoebe, daughter of Dr. W. W. Mayo, 11, 21, 33, 41, 50
— Phoebe, daughter of Dr. Will, 174, 210
— policy, 89
— Properties Association, 148, 149
— Sarah, daughter of Dr. W. W. Mayo, 11
— Dr. Thomas, 20
— Dr. William James, 9; birth of, 11, 14, 50, 53, 55, 56, 57, 58, 60, 62, 67, 70; as father's assistant, 58, 59, 64, 67, 68; breaks arm, 61; skill as horseman, 61, 62; as grade-school pupil, 63; medical education, 73; associated with father, 73; scorns "doctor's" garb, 74; self-confidence, 74; in tornado, 76-79; notice of surgical skill, 83; marriage of, 83; advanced medical training, 83; wide travels, 83, 84; on St. Mary's Hospital medical staff, 85; as hospital nurse, 88; surgical success, 90; reputation, 90; demanded best horses, 90; daring as operator, 92; first medical paper, 97; praise of brother, 98; praise of Catholic sisters, 99; seeks use for money, 100; engages investment agent, 102, 103; habits of dress, 105; appearance of, 106, 118, 209; refutes Army authority, 107; interest in poor, 109; as "universal specialist," 112; honors to, 114; chief characteristics, 118; speeds to Dr. Charlie's aid, 121-122; cites Clinic policy, 127; tribute to parents, 129; rights of brothers, 129; placed on salary, 129; treatment of poor, 131; treatment of

rich, 131, 132; creates endowment, 137, 138; serves on University of Minnesota board of regents, 138; in defense of Mayo Foundation, 140-143; commission in Army, 144; awarded Distinguished Service Medal, 147; plan of Mayo Properties Association management, 149; honesty with patients, 150; decides on larger Clinic, 151; postgraduate school open to all, 155; a surgeon's day, 157-159; claim to original techniques, 160-161, 162; known universally as Dr. Will, 165; praise of brother, 166, 167; announces retirement, 166; views on liquor, 168, 175; views on smoking, 168; views on religion, 169, 170; interest in music, 170; how to keep fit, 171; dislike for farm life, 172; as boatman, 173, 174; sells yacht for charity, 174; donates home to Foundation, 175; leader in medicine, 179; possessor of foresight, 179, 180; boomed for governor and President, 180; retirement of, 182, 188; study of cancer, 183-184; concern over increase in insanity, 185-186; criticizes education methods, 186-187; Clinic consultant, 189; makes only airplane flight, 191; praised by state officer, 195; honors father, 196; increases Foundation endowment, 197; traveled by trailer, 197; why Mayos stayed in Rochester, 198-199; cited by American Legion, 201; lauded by President Roosevelt, 203-205; given medal by medical group, 205; medicine on march, 206; health fails, 209; shocked by Dr. Charlie's death, 212; death of, 212; funeral for, 214; earnings of, 218; contribution to medical education, 219; value of estate, 219; termed medical historian, 219; honors and citations, 230-232
— Mrs. William James, 83, 172, 174, 191, 209, 212
— Dr. William Worrall, as Le Sueur homebuilder, 3, 4, 5, 9, 52; as veterinarian, 5; as copper prospector, 7, 23; as surveyor and farmer, 7; background, 7; as horseman, 9; the "old doctor," 9, 165, 196, 198, 212; as riverboat captain, 10; as Army examining surgeon, 10; Indian fighter, 13, 31, 37, 38, 52; birth of, 19; emigration to America, 20; as medical student, 20, 55; graduation from medical college, 21; marriage of, 21; operator of medical school, 21; illness of, 21; as politician, 23, 58, 72, 93, 99; near death in North Woods, 23; called to Indian war, 31; joins volunteers, 35; as surgeon to soldiers, 37, 52; appeal to volunteers, 38; at Indian hangings, 47; transfer to Rochester, 49; arrival in Rochester, 50, 126; in partnership, 52, 53; as country doctor, 53, 64; as coroner, 57, 58, 59; as mayor, 58, 72, 93; "pioneer surgeon of the Northwest," 65, 67; as medical society founder, 70, 71; attack on political foes, 72; role in tornado, 78, 79, 80, 81; as sponsor of St. Mary's Hospital, 82, 83; as head of St. Mary's medical staff, 85; concern over hospital, 87; views on hospital policy, 89; enlarges stable, 90; as a fast driver, 91; his high reputation, 92; election to state senate, 93, 99; as traveler, 99, 114, 115; activities in late years, 114; his first automobile, 115; honored when eighty-five, 116; suffers accident, 116; death of, 116; honored by Rochester, 116; purchase of lot in Rochester, 126; tribute to sons, 129; praised by grandson, 196; marker cites early deeds, 196; honored by sons, 196, 201
— Mrs. William Worrall (Louise Abigail Wright), 7, 8, 11, 12, 21, 23, 32, 33, 34, 50, 54, 55, 61, 67; organizes women's militia, 40, 41, 42, 45; as parent, 69; death of, 117
"Mayos' Folly," 127, 154
— Foundation for Medical Education and Research, 149, 155, 174, 175, 186, 197; creation of, 136, 137, 138; opposition to, 139, 142; defense of, by Dr. Will, 141-143
Mayow, John, 20
Mayowood, 164, 171, 172
Medical Officers Reserve Corps, 147
Medical Reserve Corps, 144, 147, 148
Medical school, 20, 54, 55, 64, 90, 96, 102, 110, 137; in wartime, 145; postgraduate training center, 145, 148, 155, 169, 173, 181, 186, 187, 222

Medical societies, 70, 71, 106, 114, 174, 209
Medicine, 4, 5, 8, 20, 22, 49, 53, 57, 58, 64, 66, 69, 70, 96, 128, 129, 141, 167, 181, 194, 204, 205; advancement of, 105, 125, 192; changes in, 183; in World War I, 183; preventive, 185
Mercy Hospital, Chicago, 210
Meyerding, Dr. Henry W., 139, 218
Michigan, University of, 73, 175
Microscope, 55, 56, 57, 73
Middlesex Hospital, 20
Military, 145, 146, 148, 221; commission, 46
Millet, Dr. Melvin C., 112, 139
Minneapolis, Minnesota, 174, 184, 221
— Public Health Association, 134, 187
— River, 4, 8, 24, 28, 48
— River Valley, 7, 9, 11, 14, 26, 45, 46
— State Medical Society, 70, 71, 106, 114, 209
— State of, 6, 8, 16, 17, 24, 47, 49, 57, 107, 108, 114, 150, 202, 207, 215
— University of, 96, 113, 137, 138, 139, 142, 149, 174
Missouri, University of, 21
Moes, Mother Mary Alfred, 79, 81, 82, 85, 87, 88
Money, 99, 102, 131, 132, 135, 136, 137, 143, 156, 175, 186, 219
Mother Mary Gervase, 214
Mother Samuel, 214
Murphy, Dr. John Benjamin, 110
Murphy, Monsignor Garrett P., 213
Murray, Archbishop John Gregory, 213
Myrick, Andrew J., 18, 19, 27

N

Navy Medical Corps, 145, 148
Neuralgia, 73
New Ulm, Minnesota, 195; attacked by Indians, 28, 29, 30, 31, 33, 35, 36, 37, 38, 39, 40, 43; abandonment of, 44, 45
New York, 54, 55, 74, 83, 96, 99, 107, 110, 111, 117, 121, 124, 182, 215, 222
— Postgraduate Medical School, 84
Niles Academy, 70
Notre Dame University, 213
Nuns, 82, 84, 95, 96
Nurses, 78, 88, 95, 123, 158, 174, 201; for tornado victims, 79, 80; practical, 84; in wartime, 139
Nu Sigma Nu, 222

O

O'Donnell, Rev. Hugh, 213
Olmsted County, Minnesota, 57, 91, 93, 171; Probate Court, 219
Olson, Governor Floyd B., 202
Operating table, 54, 58, 68, 86, 159, 162, 209
Osler, Sir William, 110
Ostrum, John D., 82
Ovarian tumor, 66, 92, 97
Owens College, 20
Oxygen, tent, 210

P

Parks, 116, 170
Parrant, Pierre, 22
Pasteur, Louis, 53, 54, 129, 179
Patent medicine, 73
Pathologists, 150, 159
Pathology, 113; in wartime, 145, 159
Patients, 9, 85, 86, 88, 89, 90, 92, 97, 98, 99, 101, 125, 126, 128, 132, 134, 145, 150, 151, 154, 156, 157, 158, 159, 166, 169, 170, 172, 199; fees of, 130; increase in number at St. Mary's Hospital, 135; reaction of, 165; million Clinic patients, 217
Peck, Dr. Charles H., 125
Pelvis, 162
Pfaender, Representative Albert, 195
Philanthropy, 108, 148, 153, 194, 218, 219
Physician, 78, 86, 169, 178; dress, 73, 74
Physiologist, 150
Pig's Eye Landing, 22
"Pill Hill," 218
Pills, 72
Plummer, Dr. Henry S., 112, 139
Pneumonia, 210
Politics, 57, 58, 92, 167, 180, 181, 189, 202
Polyclinic Postgraduate Medical School, 83, 84
Postgraduate studies, 55; school, 155
Post-mortem, 58, 59, 113
Presbyterian Hospital, New York, 121
President, 180, 181; of the United States, 199, 201
President, Notre Dame University, 213; of University of Minnesota, 140
Princeton University, 192
Prisoners, of Indians, 46; Indians held by Army, 46
Profession, 73, 97, 100, 108, 109, 139, 142, 154, 162, 171, 179, 192, 195, 204, 205, 207; altruism of, 141

Prohibition, 71, 168
Protestant, 94; clergyman, 211
Public health, 133, 134, 187, 195, 204

Q

Quacks, 72

R

Radiologist, 150
Rankin, Dr. Fred W., 176
Regents, University of Minnesota board of, 137, 138, 139, 142, 160, 174, 175
Reiter, Julius, 109, 115, 116
Rejuvenation, 182
Reputation, 108, 157, 159, 161, 163, 192
Research, 97, 102, 142, 149, 150, 178, 182
Rheumatism, 73
Riesman, Dr. David, 205
Riordan, Monsignor William, 71
Rochester, Minnesota, 57, 58, 60, 69, 70, 72, 74, 75, 87, 93, 97, 122, 125, 129, 147, 151, 153, 170, 198, 199, 221; as Civil War recruiting district headquarters, 49, 50; as medical center, 49, 50; tornado, 77, 78; medical interest in, 106; Mayo celebration at, 201, 209; Dr. Charlie's funeral at, 212; city named, 215; city incorporated, 216; population of, 216; business of, 216; surrounding region, 217
Rochester City Post, 52, 60, 63, 80, 93
Rochester Old Boys and Girls Association, 119, 170
Rochester Record and Union, 74, 83, 84
Roosevelt, President Franklin D., 199, 201, 202, 203-205, 211-212
Rotary International, 184
Royal College of Surgeons, 114

S

"Sage of Mininger," 57
St. Mary's Hospital, 10, 99; start of, 82; work commenced on, 84; formal opening, 85; first medical staff, 85; first nursing staff, 85; first patient, 85; as an investment, 87; success of, 88, 90; policy, 88, 89; rival hospital, 97; overcrowded, 98; addition to, 98; third operating room opened, 112; east wing added, 113; facilities outgrown, 135; largest Rochester hospital, 135, 155, 157, 162; Mary Joseph,

noted sister, dies, 209; Dr. Will undergoes operation, 210
St. Mary's School of Nursing, 208
St. Paul, Minnesota, 4, 7, 10, 22, 23, 27, 28, 47, 92, 173, 205, 213
Sawyer, Brigadier General C. E., 145
Scalpel, 68, 97, 158, 162, 188
Scientific journals, 54, 69, 96, 106, 110, 114, 173, 174
Scissors, 162
"Scrub nurse," 67, 68
See, Captain Charles H., 50
Sibley, General Henry Hastings, 45
Sidelis, Sister, 85
Sienna, Sister, 85
Sigmoid, 161
Sinsinawa Dominican Sisters, 214
Sioux Indians, 11, 12, 13, 14, 16, 25, 26, 27, 46, 48, 196
Sisters of Mount Carmel, Dubuque, Iowa, 214
Sisters of St. Francis, 80, 82, 84, 88
Sisters of the Catholic Church, 213
"Skeleton of the Mayos," 48, 49
Smoking, 168, 175, 176, 183
Smullen, Thomas, 50
Snyder, Fred B., 160
South Dakota Medical Association, 183
Southern Minnesota Medical Association, 96
— Surgical Society, 121
Spanish-American War, 183
Specialists, 150, 158, 186, 187, 218
Spine, 73
Staff members, 85, 134, 151, 155, 156, 165, 166, 174, 198, 214
Standards, 97, 110, 113, 133, 169, 204
Stark, Mrs. Jacob, 92
Start, Judge Charles M., 74
Sterilizer, 67, 68
Stethoscope, 53
Stinchfield, Dr. Augustus White, 92, 96
Stomach, 158, 162, 184
Student, 73, 102, 137, 139; assistant, 73
"Supreme Court of Condemned Patients," 218
Surgeon, 78, 86, 88, 90, 106, 108, 127, 219; European, 84; general, 155
Surgery, 37, 51, 54, 55, 68, 69, 73, 106, 128, 129, 204; in tornado, 79; skill of Dr. Will, 83; in hotel, 84; advance of, 90, 95; development of, 96; specialties, 96, 97, 98; gall bladder, 110; preponderance of, 112; on Dr. Charlie, 121, 124; transition of, 130; in wartime, 145; increase in, 151, 157; skill in, 158; abdominal, 158, 160; ethical level of, 179; early, 183

Surgical mortality, 90, 98, 99
— needle, 60, 68
— pavilion, 135
— training, 73
"Surgical twins," 125, 212
Suture, 67, 160
Sylvester, Sister, 85

T

Technique, 91, 92, 160, 162, 178
Temperance, 168
"The Chief," 165, 197, 198
Thyroid gland, 91, 112
Tobacco, 174, 177
Tornado, 77; toll of, 78; emergency
    hospital, 79; volunteer nurses, 79;
    surgery, 79
Tousley, G. M., 4, 7
Traverse de Sioux, Minnesota, 29, 30,
    33
Treatment, 91, 128, 131, 145, 150, 157,
    162; early, 182, 183; of cancer,
    184; of Dr. Will, 209
Trenholm, George, 176
Tumors, 66, 92, 97, 159, 162, 172, 184

U

Ulcer, 162, 209, 210
United States, 91, 139, 143, 155, 185,
    186, 197
United States Army Medical Corps, 146
— Senate, 16
— Steel Corporation, 23
Universalist, 98
"Universal Specialist," 112
University of Havana, 190
— Manchester, 20, 196, 197
— Michigan, 73, 175, 208, 222
— Minnesota, 96, 113, 137, 138, 139,
    142, 149, 160, 174; medical school,
    139, 155

— Missouri, 21
— Pennsylvania, 96, 192
Ureter, 162
Urology, 112

V

Veins, varicose, 162
"Veritas," 72
Veterinarian, 96
Vincent, Dr. George E., 140
Vision, 150

W

Waggoner, Jacob, 65, 66, 67; Mrs.
    Jacob, 65, 66, 67
Walters, Dr. Waltman, 174, 210
Walters, Mayo, 201
War, 139, 143, 144, 148, 222; veterans
    of, 201; memorial, 202
Warman, Dr. F. Guy, 196
Washington University, 21
Webster, Judd, 26
Whisky, 71
Will, 219
Williamson, Rev. Thomas S., 17, 19
Wilson, Dr. Louis B., 139, 159, 161
Witherstine, Mayor H. H., 98
"Wonder of the West," 220
World War I, 144, 154, 205

X

X-ray plates, 172

Y

Yankton College, South Dakota, 190,
    197
Young Women's Christian Association,
    Rochester, 222

ABOUT THE AUTHOR

ADOLPH REGLI was born in Eau Clair, Wisconsin, graduated from the University of Wisconsin and then embarked on a newspaper career which took him to New York, Florida, California and Minnesota. When the last paper he worked for was sold and he was out of a job, he decided to continue with his writing, this time as an author of books. He opened a small business and devoted his evening hours to writing. Biography particularly interested him and in time he established himself as an author of books for young people.